SINGLED OUT FOR

PREPARATION

EMBRACING THE MOST IMPORTANT SEASON OF YOUR LIFE

AZLAN WILLIAMS

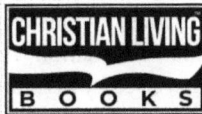

CHRISTIAN LIVING
B O O K S

Largo, MD

Christian Living Books, Inc.
We bring your dreams to fruition.
ChristianLivingBooks.com

ISBN 97815622965790

CONTENTS

DEDICATION

I dedicate this book to a few different people. Of course, I want to honor my Lord and Savior Jesus Christ. I thank Him for dying on the cross for me, my sins, and the opportunity to be free. I am grateful and blessed that I made the choice to accept Him into my life and for receiving the gift of the Holy Spirit.

I want to dedicate this book to my parents, Douglas Williams and Rhonda Williams. I thank you mom for continuing to love me and raise me into a Godfearing man. I thank you for showing me Jesus and always praying for me and being the great supporter, mother, and friend that you have been. You are one of the most talented people I know, and I pray that you continue to walk in your purpose and be everything that God has called you to be. To my dad, Dougie Fresh, who is no longer with us but in the heavenly place enjoying Jesus, thank you for being the best dad a son could ask for! Thank you for being my father, my coach, my friend, and my motivation. I miss you dearly and I thank you for showing me how to fight and not give up and do what needed to be done.

To my grandparents, Ronnie and Jackie Calloway, thank you for being the example of how to place your trust in God and to base your relationship off the word of God and never sway. Pop Pop, thank you for showing me how to be a man and take care of my responsibilities and paying attention. Gi Gi, thank you for always believing in me and being one of the greatest blessings I will ever receive in life.

To my brother Anthony Cotton, the man of his word, thank you for being a friend, a brother, an example and being one of the hardest working people I know. To my other brothers, Conrad, and Talan, thank y'all for always believing in me and pushing me on the court and in life.

To Kaihlani, I am so blessed to be in your life, and I pray that God will bless you and keep you for your entire life. You have parents who will love you always and know if you need anything, Uncle Azlan will always be here for you! And to all my family and friends, thank you for believing in me and seeing the best in me even when I didn't see it in myself! I LOVE YOU ALL!

INTRODUCTION

T AKE THIS FROM SOMEONE who literally, every day for about eight years, wondered why they were still single. This is a book that will change your perspective on singleness, and how this is the most important stage of life you will be experiencing. I was one who preached trusting in God, screamed from the mountaintops that God was my source, told everyone around me how much God loved them and how He is always on time. However, I was not completely living it myself. See, deep down I was always wondering when it would be my time to have love.

I always binged my chick flicks, listened to all the slow jams, and wrote all the love poems. As I recently found all those poems, I had to ask myself "What in the world was I thinking and where was I at?" I laugh now because I see how deep I was trying to be, but I also thank God for getting me out of that stage of life where I was so sad and to be honest, depressed! I put my completion and hope in how women saw me and could "potentially" treat me as opposed to putting my hope in God and relying on the Holy Spirit to fulfill me.

I am now 29 years old and can say I am just now embracing my singleness. I soon realized that God has a plan for me that can only be accomplished and completed if I am alone. After taking care of my dad for years, taking care of my grandpa when he became ill, and just wanting to help everyone I could, I have to be honest: I always wondered when the time would come when the same effort I gave would be returned. Even in the situationships I was a part of, I felt as if I gave more effort than I received. But see, I was trusting more in the person as opposed to trusting in God. I would get into things that I didn't ask God about. I just did it because I felt lonely and wanted companionship when I had the greatest companion right there next to me trying to get my attention. I had to face the brutal truth; I was not ready to be in a relationship.

The relationship that I already had and needed to focus on was taking a backseat and nothing worked. I wanted to do what I thought was right and how I thought it should work. After watching the "Relationship Goals: Reloaded" by Pastor Michael Todd of Transformation Church, my whole idea and plan was changed. I finally decided that I would trust in the Lord to guide my relationships and ultimately my entire life.

The Holy Spirit revealed to me that I had fallen in love with the idea of relationship, having a girlfriend, and marriage as opposed to falling in love with the preparation and journey of becoming first, a Godly man, and then a husband. I hadn't enjoyed being by myself and learning who God needs me to be. Also, the thing that really held me back from progressing was looking at everyone else and their relationships and how they came together. I had an idea of when I would be married, how I got married, and who I would be married to. Those ideas took priority over who God says I am, what my dreams and goals were, how I would become a husband,

and what God needed me to do in this season of singleness. It all came down to the simple fact that if I am not doing what I am supposed to be doing in my singleness with God, the future will not be as progressive as it should because I am going backwards. When I get married, it will be twice as hard to do what I need to do because now I have someone else to focus on and make a priority.

When you're single and you have more time to focus on things, God also speaks to you more and you have more space to listen. I believe this book will truly help whoever reads this to embrace their single season and to be completely dedicated to it. God wants to do a work in you so great while it's just you and Him. He wants to show you how to be successful in all you do. He wants to spend all the time with you and give you business ideas, extra money, extra peace, and the foundation of relationship with Him that will get you thru anything that tries to come against you.

At the end of this book, you will understand the importance of your single season and how it paves the way for every situation in your life; now and forever! Allow the Holy Spirit to speak to your heart, show you the truth, and heal your heart so you can receive the desires of your heart.

1

WHY AM I STILL SINGLE?

OR ANYONE WHO IS single and not in a relationship, I can almost guarantee that you have asked this question or at least wondered it: Why am I single? Today, we are bombarded with all types of different relationships. We see the relationships of Russell Wilson and Ciara, Jay Z and Beyonce, Steph and Ayesha Curry, and we begin to think how we would love a relationship that models theirs. One of the trendiest topics or most used words today is "Relationship Goals!" It's very easy to look at something and desire it, especially if it looks good or promising.

I remember in high school when I would literally sit in class and daydream about being in a relationship. I mean I was a good basketball player, I got good grades, a lot of people liked me, and shoot I thought I was cute. I just felt like if I had the finest girl to be on my side, I would be *the man*, I would be complete. I truly thought I was the whole package and that anybody who chose me would be the luckiest girl on earth.

As time continued to go by, I had flings and had a few interests, but nobody seemed to want to commit to me. I had become sad and thought to myself, "why does nobody want to be with me?" The sadness turned into depression and the depression turned into being desperate. I was 16 years old and feeling like I was missing out on everything! My teammates used to clown me for being a virgin and I began to feel the weight of the world on my shoulders for being different.

It was the summer of 2010 and I had just finished up my sophomore year in high school. I had an amazing year in basketball and even made a name for myself on the court. This would be an important summer coming up in the AAU circuit for I was ready to take on all the best players in the country. I had big hopes that colleges would start noticing me and I had all the confidence in the world that I would get someone's attention. Little did I know that a week before my team and I would head to LA, someone was about to catch my attention.

FOCUS CAN BE DANGEROUS

One summer night, a couple of my friends were throwing a house party. My parents didn't really let me go out too much, but this night they gave me the ok. I remember holding up the wall like a lot of us guys do and just kind of scoping who was there. I remember seeing a familiar face and as I went over to speak and say hello, she had a friend. The friend spoke and said, "Oh man, he is so cute!" That is all I had to hear.

When you get desperate, anything positive sounds and looks good. I made myself feel lonely. I told myself that nobody liked me so much to where I believed it. So, this compliment comes and I feel like I just hit the lotto. I was snatched and my attention and focus immediately switched to the young lady. Not only was I so hung over on the compliment, but the young lady was very beautiful. So, you know I felt like I was the man for real!

The point I want to make here is that when you are not in a place of focus on God, any and everything can take your focus. Focus can be dangerous depending on what you're focusing on. My focus had shifted from the upcoming basketball trips, to what this young lady

> *When you get desperate, anything positive sounds and looks good.*

had said to me and how I could get to know her. The crazy part is, my focus became so fixed on her that night, danger could've showed itself and I had lost all my care about my whereabouts and more importantly my discernment. My only goal that night was to get the digits and I didn't care what else happened. I had to get the number.

Another point I want to make, regarding us guys; when a man wants something, he will do whatever he can to make sure it happens. That is naturally built in us men. We are made to make things happen and made to G.I.B.A.M (Get It By Any Means). That's also what society teaches us. It's what our uncles at the family BBQ's taught us and even some of our own fathers have taught us to tame our desires. In the church, we were told not to have sex before marriage and that was it. They never really gave us a why or the meaning of covenant or the consequences of not waiting.

However, I can say that I was not one of those kids! I was taught and learned at a young age why I should not have sex before marriage. My church had an amazing woman by the name of Andrea Mosby-Jones come and give a course on W.A.I.T. Training which stands for (Why Am I Tempted). She gave amazing examples of why you should wait until you get married to have sex, the consequences of having sex out of marriage, and the potential things you could face and deal with if you make the choice to have sex out of marriage.

My grandfather also always told me that when you do things God's way that everything is better. My grandparents were married for 28 years, got a divorce and were apart for 7 years, and then got re-married and long story short, lived happily and blessed until the passing of my grandfather at the end of 2020. My grandfather would always share with me how much better the second marriage was because he submitted to God and lead the marriage with God at the helm. He said not only was the marriage and bond better but other things were better too! I always admired the time spent with my Pop Pop because it was full of stories but more importantly full of wisdom and learning.

> *You only get scared or try to be secretive when you know you're not supposed to be doing something.*

So, you can see, I was warned, I was encouraged to do the right thing, I was surrounded and drenched in support. I knew right from wrong, and I knew when I was in a place I shouldn't have been in. In a lot of situations, we have a choice and ladies and gents, I made the wrong decision.

TRADING THE V CARD FOR A DEBIT CARD

After the tournament was over, all I could think about was getting back to Denver to see the young lady I had been talking to. I had a decent trip and I played alright, but my focus was on getting back to see her. Anxious feelings arose as I was on my way to see her. I wasted no time and called my brother to take me since I had no car at the time and no driver's license. I knew what was about to happen and so I thought, I was ready for it!

4

As I am writing this, I realized how much sin sex can cause and I am not talking about just actually having sex. I lied to my parents and told them I was going to the movies. I had to be secretive. I mean like c'mon, who's really going to tell their parents, "Hey mom and dad, I am going to lose my virginity. I'll be back around 11." You only get scared or try to be secretive when you know you're not supposed to be doing something.

> *The woman was convinced. She saw that the tree was beautiful and its fruit looked delicious, and she wanted the wisdom it would give her. So she took some of the fruit and ate it. Then she gave some to her husband, who was with her, and he ate it too. At that moment their eyes were opened, and they suddenly felt shame at their nakedness. So they sewed fig leaves together to cover themselves. When the cool evening breezes were blowing, the man and his wife heard the Lord God walking about in the garden. So they hid from the Lord God among the trees. Then the Lord God called to the man, "Where are you?* (Genesis 3:6-9 NLT)

This scripture has so much revelation and conviction in it because prior in Genesis Chapter 2 and verse 25 it says:

> *Now the man and his wife were both naked, but they felt no shame.* (Genesis 2:25 NLT)

Now back to Chapter 3 when Adam and Eve realized they were naked, verse 10 says:

> *The man replied, "I heard you walking in the garden, so I hid. I was afraid because I was naked." Who told you that you were naked?" the Lord God asked.* (Genesis 3:10 NLT)

God knew that the only way they would've felt shame is if they did exactly what God told them not to do. The ONE AND ONLY RULE, in the Garden of Eden was to not eat from this one tree. Just one tree! They had the freedom of everything else in the garden. But the one thing that was looking desirable, also is where satan dwelled. The devil had convinced Eve that if she ate from the tree, that she would be wise and be like God. See satan was kicked out of heaven because he thought he was greater than God. Ever hear the saying "misery loves company?" Well, that's exactly what the devil tries to do every single day.

I thought because I was a virgin and everyone around me was having sex, that's what I needed to do, or that's what I was missing out on. I gave up my "innocence" and what I held dearly for so long and what I thought was special in my eyes. I allowed what I thought I was missing out on to withdraw from who I was and who God said I was. After the act, I felt like I was in overdraft and as if I had made the biggest mistake of my life. I had traded my V card for a debit card, but this was a feeling I didn't believe I could get out of overdraft.

GENERATIONAL CURSES

Although I had been taught why it was important to wait until you got married to have sex, I still made the decision to have sex anyways. It was not all my fault as to why I was introduced to sex. I was introduced to sex at a very young age. I was molested and shown things by an older female cousin. I also found something a lot of us have experienced that has really messed us up, pornography. I would find my dad's videos in the basement when I was looking for Michael Jordan tapes so I could work on my basketball moves. At the time, I didn't know exactly what I was looking at. I

6

just remember having a weird feeling and I just knew that it wasn't right. Although, I wouldn't be interested in that till years later, the seed had been planted in my mind and the curiosity was there.

I always take responsibility for my actions, but we must understand that some things are not our fault. We can't always control how we are introduced to things. I think about how I was introduced to what I would consider, the biggest roadblock of my life, and how I would be embarrassed and felt shame if I was the reason as to why my kids were introduced to porn or anything out of God's will. I know how debilitating it was to me and that's the last thing I would want my kids to go through.

Up to about early 2020, porn was still an issue and a roadblock in my life. I wondered why it was such an issue and why I wanted to get rid of it but just seemed as if I couldn't. A good friend of mine shared with me a few chapters in Romans that would forever change my life.

> *Because of the weakness of your human nature, I am using the illustration of slavery to help you understand all this. Previously, you let yourselves be slaves to impurity and lawlessness, which led ever deeper into sin. Now you must give yourselves to be slaves to righteous living so you will become holy.* (Romans 6:19 TPT)

As you can see, I had made myself a slave to lust, porn, masturbation, and looking at women lustfully. Although I wanted to do right, it was a feeling of being chained to the lust. I felt that I would never be able to get free from it. Having a relationship with God and always asking to be free, what I realized is that I had focused more on the sin in my heart instead of focusing on the healing power of the Holy Spirit to help me out.

Don't you realize that your body is the temple of the Holy
Spirit, who lives in you and was given to you by God? You
do not belong to yourself, for God bought you with a high
price. So you must honor God with your body.

(1 Corinthians 6:19 NLT)

You see, I didn't value my body the way God does. I sought validation from lust. Every single time when I thought it would provide some type of satisfaction, I was left feeling empty and useless. So many times, we are trying so hard not to sin and that's what becomes our focus. What we fail to realize or remember is that when you accepted Jesus into your life, the sin, the lust, the addictions, the pain, the hurt, anything that has held you back, is already taken care of because Jesus died on the cross. When He died on the cross, when He said, "IT IS FINISHED". That included all your sins and mistakes. The same grace and mercy that was provided to your parents and ancestors as well. Whether they did the work or not to become free from their bondage is one thing. Again, the truth is that some things that happen to us are not our fault. Where it becomes our fault is if we continue to live in the bondage we have already acknowledged and asked God to forgive us for. When we ask God to forgive us, He has already forgotten what you did. Too many times we ask God to forgive us and then try to go back and pick up what we "left" at the feet of God.

Pour out all your worries and stress upon Him and
leave them there, for He always tenderly cares for you.

(1 Peter 5:7 TPT)

God wants your problems, worries, your anxious feelings, your struggles and your pain. He wants to be able to release the ropes we have been tied by and heal the brands of sin we have been burned with. We must leave the problems there, repent and not turn back.

Again, we must allow God and the help of the Holy Spirit to guide us through all journeys of life. A problem I had was I was so in love with the idea of being in a relationship and wanting to be married but I was not in love with the journey of preparation. I remember when the Holy Spirit told me that I needed to embrace my single season and if you could see my face; it was as if I just heard the most confusing, no sense having, comment I've ever heard. "I have been single almost my entire life. What do you mean embrace my singleness? I think I've embraced it long enough!" This is how the rest of the conversation went between me and my flesh and the Holy Spirit and His wisdom…

Me: What do you mean? I've been single and I've been doing fine so how am I not embracing my singleness?

Holy Spirit: You have been focused on what is to come as opposed to where you are at right now.

Me: But aren't I supposed to have a vision of where I want to be and what I want to desire?

Holy Spirit: Yes, however you are doing things out of place. You are trying to be a husband and you aren't even a boyfriend or a friend. You are reading books about how to keep a wife when you don't even know who your wife will be. You are praying for things outside of your season. And more importantly God has things for you to do for Him that you won't be able to accomplish with someone. He won't be able to manifest it through you if you're focus is somewhere else.

Me: Well, how do I get prepared for the journey and focus on me in this single season?

Holy Spirit: By focusing on Me! By inviting Me in! By trusting in Me! Just try it.

As you can see, I thought with the little knowledge I had gained, that I could handle anything that came my way and that I would just attach the Lord to it. Dating without asking God should I pursue the young lady was one thing. Sleeping around without acknowledging the Holy Spirit being right there in the room and bed with me is another thing. Putting my own pleasure and "needs" in front of the Lord is the wrong thing. I was saying that He isn't enough. And, my selfish and impure actions and thoughts made that evident.

A question that comes up often is why. Why am I still single God? Why is this person in a relationship and I'm not? Why do I keep trying to make this work and it's going nowhere? Why can't this person see my worth? How in the world did they get someone that looks like that? C'mon we have thought that once, or maybe twice. The why I want to propose to you is this: when you see nothing you have tried has worked, why won't you give God the chance to not only fix and heal but place you in the best place possible? You may not know how to start but I can tell you it begins with repentance and forgiving yourself. In the next chapter, we will go over what is your why and how God must be right in the middle of everything you do. If you don't know what your why is, be prepared to hear from the Holy Spirit!

2

WHAT IS MY WHY?

F OR THE LONGEST TIME, I would always try to find motivation in something, shoot anything I could. I would think if more people doubted me, that would light a fire under my butt. I felt as if I got attention from multiple women, that would give me motivation. I felt that if I got the recognition from people on how good of a basketball player I was, that would fill me up.

As I continued to do what I thought was good and fulfilling, I soon realized that the way I was going about it was not working at all. I was putting my reliance in things that couldn't fill me up. My fallback plan was a destructive net. I had the mindset that if one girl would give up on me that I could just go find another. I had the Gucci Mane mindset, "Girls are like buses, miss one next 15 one coming." You see, us men are taught in society that we should not commit and "live our best life." A lot of us are taught that we should sleep with whoever we want, sow our wild oats, don't cry, live your life. But what does live your life really mean? Why do you do the things you do?

I followed a false narrative of G.I.B.A.M (Get It By Any Means) but using it for all aspects of my life. Women show me interest, get it by any means. Chase the fame of being a good ball player, get it by any means. Promote myself and make sure people know my name and see every good deed I am doing, get it by any means. Grinding toward an unfulfilling destination leaves you dried out and tired. I fought harder to gain the attention and push toward promoting my name. However, that left me feeling empty.

> *Grinding toward an unfulfilling destination leaves you dried out and tired.*

I had no real why! I would use God as a sticky note to attach Him to my plans but not make Him the foundation. I think of all the times God saved me from situations that I thought I wanted and even tried to force myself into. Most of the time it's because the situation (she) looked good. Even in basketball, I was so dedicated to it that it was my god. You see, I had a plan and I was going to make sure I saw it through!

> *Within your heart you can make plans for your future, but the Lord chooses the steps you take to get there.*
> (Proverbs 16:9 TPT)

Have you ever tried to grind your way to the plans that you made but come up short every time? It just seems like nothing that you are doing is working. (Both hands raise). You see, although I was raised around very wise people and one would consider themselves to be wise, there is no wisdom, no knowledge, no experience, and no success without the Lord. When I thought I had a master plan, God could be laughing at it.

For the "foolish" things of God have proven to be wiser than human wisdom. And the "feeble" things of God have proven to be far more powerful than any human ability.

(1 Corinthians 1:25 TPT)

TRUE DELIGHT AND FORGIVENESS

Delight thyself also in the Lord; And he shall give thee the desires of thine heart. (Psalm 37:4 NLT)

I am going to give you the version from the The Passion Translation which states, "Find your delight and true pleasure in Yahweh (God), and He will give you what you desire most."

Now I can't move forward if we do not know what that word, desire means. In the *Webster's Dictionary* the definition for desire is "to long or hope for." (I am big on definitions because of my grandfather. Shout out to POP POP).

The truth is, I longed for a relationship, boyfriend and girlfriend type, more than I longed for my relationship with Jesus. I hoped that someone would like me and want to commit to me, more than laying my hope in the One who already committed to me. I remember one time I went above and beyond for a young lady. I would go out of my way, I would do things that I usually wouldn't do for anybody. And, I felt as if I did everything in a decent way. However, the one thing I didn't do was ask God how to go about it. Also, I didn't ask God if I should even pursue the young lady.

The one thing that I have learned is that if you do things out of order and out of God's timing, you can not only damage yourself but the other person as well. You could even put yourself into a situation that leaves you worse off than you were before. God is a God of strategy and wisdom. I had to realize that although I felt I was ready to be in a relationship, I wasn't. I was an impatient, my way or the highway type boy. There were things that I didn't put up with that were minor and didn't give anybody the chance to make it right. What I lacked in my own life was the one thing that is extremely important and will set you free. To some people it's a word that you can become offended by, and that word is Forgiveness.

Later Peter approached Jesus and said, "How many times do I have to forgive my fellow believer who keeps offending me? Seven times?" Jesus answered, "Not seven times, Peter, but seventy times seven times! (Matthew 18:21-22 TPT)

You see, Peter was like a lot of us. He was stubborn, wanted to know everything, but also very loyal. Peter was not perfect and even though you can say Peter was like a teacher's pet with Jesus, he still had his faults. We are often told that we must forgive. Many times, growing up I thought that I had to forgive people for their sake. The truth is we need to forgive for our own sake. Time for a few definitions.

- Forgive: to cease to feel resentment against an offender
- Forgiveness: the act of forgiving
- Forgiving: allowing room for error or weakness, or willing or able to forgive

So, you see, there are levels to this forgiveness thing. It's one thing to forgive. It's another thing to show forgiveness. It's another thing to be forgiving. Let's see if I can break this down for you. Forgive and forgiveness are in the same boat. When you forgive someone, you show an act of forgiveness. As the definition said, you cease to feel resentment toward one who offended you. Let's stop right there for a moment. There are many ways we can be offended. Some are legit reasons to take offense, and some are because we picked up the offense. There have been situations some of us have gone thru that weren't our fault and we had no choice. Some of those situations being rape, molestation, sexual harassment, domestic violence, and addictions. Let me be the first to say, I am truly sorry, and I pray you receive the healing that you need in order to move forward in your life to live a life of freedom and not bondage.

I was one of those people who has dealt with being molested at a young age. I will never speak of anything I have no experience or knowledge in and so again, I am sorry. One of the things that was hard for me to overcome was the reality of accepting that it WAS NOT my fault. I didn't know what I was doing and although the other person did, the one person who saw me at the time was God. Now many of you might be confused and ask why God would allow something like that to happen. One thing that many people may not understand is that the enemy is working hard to use the people that will carry out his plan of diversion, perversion, and just straight up sickness.

> *I don't know what I'm thinking, I'm just frustrated.*
> *I don't mean to question you, I'm just confused.*
> *I don't know what else to do, I've been patient and it sucks waiting.*
> *Took my mans from me, that forever hurts.*
> *But puttin' the blame on you, that'd never work.*
> *I know this ain't your fault, it's the devils work!*
> — Joyner Lucas

I put this part of the song in the book because he is someone who is lost and doesn't understand why things happen. They are questioning God on how things happen and why they happen. I don't believe it's wrong to question God. If anybody is to be questioned, it should be Him. He will give you the answers for how to become healed. Bad things happen all the time. Bad things happen to good people. However, it is not God's will to have bad things happen to anyone. We must know and understand that God is grieved when things happen to His kids. He cries when you cry, and He mourns because you mourn. I say all of this to say that God will get you out of any situation that you need help out of.

I will be the one to say that forgiveness is not easy. I must ask the Holy Spirit daily to show me if there is any way in me that is wrong, displeasing to Him, and what unforgiveness I am holding hostage in my heart. Holding onto pain and resentment is a faster way to leave this earth. Having things in your heart that you don't know about can be dangerous and very draining to your soul.

> God, I invite your searching gaze into my heart. Examine me through and through; find out everything that may be hidden within me. Put me to the test and sift through all my anxious cares. See if there is any path of pain I'm walking on, and lead me back to your glorious, everlasting way – the path that brings me back to you. (Psalm 139:23-24 TPT)

One of the problems we as people face is we want the whole thing to be healed and not have to do the work. There are times when God completely heals you and your heart to where you don't feel any pain or unforgiveness toward someone. However, forgiveness takes work, dedication, and consistency. I am staying on this topic because without forgiveness, I truly don't believe you will be able to move forward and live your life in peace. Now, you can move forward but it won't be in peace and comfort.

I remember how I would always dwell on the things that people did to me and how messed up it was. Although I had moved on, I had not forgiven them and allowed it to stay hidden in my heart. Maybe that person did do something dirty and messed up to me, that was not

Holding onto pain and resentment is a faster way to leave this earth.

the ultimate problem at that point. The problem became a problem when I didn't move forward and I hadn't forgiven *myself* for putting me through those trying times. Again, there are situations that are out of our control. There are situations where we don't know how to get out of them. Then there are situations that we have stayed in where we know it wasn't good for us, but we felt we were good enough to change the other person. We saw the potential and not the reality.

POTENTIAL VS. REALITY

The word potential is dangerous, straight up! I know growing up, being a basketball player, that word potential is tossed around and used strongly and lightly. In sports, you hear that word often.

Potential means 1. having or showing the capacity to become or develop into something in the future (adjective). 2. latent qualities or abilities that may be developed and lead to future success or usefulness (noun)

When you have potential, you could progress or digress! No matter what end of the stick you end up on, it's still potential. We are going to go through 3 different types of potential. By the end of the demonstration, you should be able to tell which one you have been and which ones you surround yourself with.

STAGNANT POTENTIAL

This is the level of potential where the person seems to have all the upside potential in the world but hasn't moved forward in Lord knows how long. This level of potential usually does more talking than action. They have big dreams and have passions, but they just seem to be stuck. This person also has great ideas but tends to want to do more off someone then making it happen themselves. Motivation comes few and far in between and when motivated, gets a lot done, but when not motivated can be stagnant for quite some time. Everyone around this person can see the "potential" but it's hard for them to see it with in themselves. This person also will start a bunch of things but won't finish it. This person has many unfinished projects and ideas. I know this level because this level was me for a very long time.

Let's switch gears here for a second. In the dating stage, potential is very necessary. There must be potential there for it to work or not work. One of the things my grandpa told me every day was "pay attention." So let me say this: if you are paying attention when you are going on a first date with someone, or even the second or third, IF you are paying attention, you will be able to label and diagnose the potential of that person. Again, I do want to be realistic. I do know that there are some professional cons out there and people who make it seem like they are interested and run game very well.

Social media does that very well as far as making someone seem like something they are not. It's not just social media. People do it in person as well. You ever see someone who has it all? The money, the cars, the houses, the "friends", or as we like to say living our best lives. The question I do always ask is do they *really* have it all? I have seen so many people who "have it all" and take their own lives. So, to the one who has it all or seems like they have it all, another question I propose is do you have the Holy Spirit?

HOW YOU DON'T WASTE TIME

This part is mainly for my overthinkers. The ones who must analyze and break down every single part of every situation. I do have an answer for you! The answer to all your questions is the Holy Spirit. The Holy Spirit will show you exactly what to do, where to go, what not to do, and everything else that you need. There would be many times in my life when I could feel the Holy Spirit speak to me, but I would ignore it because I thought what I knew was best. This ties back to not being submitted to God and what He was telling me to do. It was not because He didn't want me to have it, but because He was protecting me.

When you are stagnant, it's because you try to figure out everything on your own. You must have so many options or you need to see results in order to know you are doing the right thing. The term "hardheaded" is joined at the hip with this type of person. I remember when I would do something and it didn't work but I would keep doing it. My dad would say "boy, why are you so hardheaded?" The way it was described to me was it's like running your head into a brick wall thinking you can break down the wall. So, you see this wall, it's very sturdy, and it has not fallen, even if the wall was shot up with bullets. This also goes under the definition of insanity, which as Albert Einstein puts it, "doing the same thing over and over again and expecting a different result."

When you are stagnant, it's because you try to figure out everything on your own.

Being stagnant can cause major insanity. In my time of doing things my way, I would truly begin to think I was crazy. In the relationships or situationships that I formed, I would always think it was me. Whether I did anything wrong or not, the enemy specializes in insanity and confusion. How many times have you seen

> *We saw the potential and not the reality.*

people go back to the same situation that caused pain, hurt, and confusion? I would go all out of my way to make sure this person knew that I am different and that I do care about them. They would show me who they are and what mindset they were in and shoot, would even tell me they didn't want me! However, I was determined to show that I was worth it and that I was all that in a bottle of hot sauce.

In spending all that energy, time, and feelings, I had the God of the universe, the love of Christ, and the help of the Holy Spirit sitting right there showing me how worth it I was. I say all of this to say, you don't have to be stagnant and do it your way. The Holy Spirit is right there to give you all the guidance and help that you need. All you must do is ask God to receive the Holy Spirit and He will give it to you. This here is the best gift you can receive. The same spirit that lived in Jesus can live in you too.

> *Yes, God raised Jesus to life! And since God's Spirit of Resurrection lives in you, He will also raise your dying body to life by the same Spirit that breathes life into you!*
> (Romans 8:11 TPT)

Today, just ask God to receive the Holy Spirit and allow the spirit of God to just flow through you. Allow the Spirit to guide you in ways that you don't know where you're going, or how you will get there. Allow the Spirit to show you who should be in your life and who shouldn't be. Trust me, He will show you. I will say this: once the Spirit reveals to you the things you ask for, after that, if you continue to do what God told you not to do, at that point it's on you. Don't be mad at God because you went back to what He delivered you from.

Part of moving forward and figuring out what your why is, is taking responsibility for your actions. If they are actions that do not honor God, then give Him the pain, the hurt, the consistency in sin, and the forgiveness of yourself. When you went to college, you chose a major. Well, this is what God majors in: taking all your problems, hurts, pains, mistakes, and mishaps. When He sent His only son Jesus to die on the cross, He took all that with Him. Our prosperity and healing are already paid for. The question is: when will you walk in it?

DIGRESSIVE POTENTIAL

This person lives in the potential of negativity. It can seem as if the person just will never get it together and is always moving in the wrong direction. There may be flashes of positivity but overall, this person is just always negative. The main problem with this person is, they always want someone to come along and join their misery and negativity. They can't deal with their problems on their own; they must find others who feel the same way they do and then try to get the masses to join their negative religion. The ultimate problem with the one who has digressive potential is that they truly have no hope.

I used to try to be as positive as I could, but when the opportunity of being negative presented itself, I would dive headfirst in it. Go big or go home, right? I truly wanted someone to feel sorry for me. I had been through a lot. Yes, my feelings were valid, but they were not for someone else to fill the void. When I would fail at something, you would've thought the world was about to end and I had been diagnosed with a terminal illness and had three hours to live. I say that to say this; NOBODY wants to be a part of negativity!

How many times have you been at work or at school and there is just that one person who can't seem to ever say or do anything positive? You ask the person "how are you today?" They respond with their whole life story of how it got started and how it's going today. By the time they finish, they have talked up your whole lunch break and you barely ate your food. Now let me be clear about myself; if there is food in front of me, I am eating it. Doesn't mean I am not listening, but a light skin must eat. There are people who do need to vent and there are people who just like to talk and hear themselves. When I come across those type of people, I always ask myself, what have they gone through to get to the point of no hope.

A LACK OF RESPONSIBILITY

The digressive person usually has gone through some things. They might have experienced a lot of traumas growing up, maybe later in life, or maybe they just choose to be negative and bitter. One thing I have learned is you cannot progress when you are putting the blame on everyone and everything else. As we stated in Chapter 1, not everything is your fault. However, how you move on and heal from it—or not heal or move on from it—is your fault. This is not to try to minimize the hurt, the pain, and the wounds from what happened to you, but God has something so much greater for you then you can ever imagine. You might be thinking at this moment, "Well Azlan, you have no idea what I have been through and what it does to me!" And you know what, you're right. I will never know because we all are different people and we all have gone down different paths. But, if I see the torment that it has brought you and the pain you can't get over, why would I want to know what you have gone through?

There are things that I have been brought through and delivered from that I don't wish anybody to experience! These are shoes you don't want to walk in. If someone could walk in your lowest and darkest shoes, would you really want them to? And I'll say this if you do, there is much forgiving on your part to be had. The Holy Spirit will show you those deep wounds, those bitter feelings, those feelings of revenge in your heart. Ask Him to show you that way you can move forward in life and not be the negative Nancy that everyone tries to avoid.

THE COMPANY YOU KEEP

This a problem that many people have; trying to fix someone. There have been times I have kept company and yes, they were negative. Just seemed like no matter what you would do or say, it would not change their mind. I've heard people say that they were going to be negative and that's just how it is. Those type of people are what I like to call either 'energy drainers' or 'time takers.' When you're around those who are negative, it really does drain your energy. After dealing with people like that, it's like you can go take a nap for 5 hours. Whether you believe it or not, it can rub off on you if you keep it around long enough.

The people you surround yourself with are HUGE! I remember my grandpa telling me that if I am the smartest or the wisest in my group of company, that I might want to find another group. He wasn't saying that the other people I surround myself with aren't smart, what he was saying was that you never want to limit yourself and just be in a group of people who don't want to get smarter or wiser.

I think about "Boyz In The Hood" and how the same friends who were around each other for years did the same exact thing every single day. Stay on the porch and smoke and drink and pretty much wait for trouble. There were only two that had "potential" and were trying to live up to it as best as they could. In the movie, Ricky, was a great football player and had a future in that. While he was doing what he could to make it to college, he still hung around his brother and other friends who were in the digressive state of life and didn't want to do anything about it. Ultimately, the company Ricky kept got him killed and left his kid without a father, mother without a son, and friends without their friend.

Why do I tell this story? The company you keep can get you in a lot of trouble and can kill you. It might not actually take your life, but it can kill your dreams and goals and aspirations and take you off the path that God originally has for you. Too many times you see a young man or a young woman who seemed like they had the world ahead of them. A few years down the road they are not in a good place. You begin to wonder, what happened to them? Here is one of the last things I will say about digressive potential. You never know what someone's story is. You always hear about billionaires taking their own lives. You hear about people who made it but then lost their lives to drugs or addictions. There was a grind toward something that would never be able to fill them up. A lot of the time when you seek validation from the outside, the ones who are hopeless are great recruiters and amazing scouts. The pit of misery is a hopeless, faithless, but comfortable place to be.

You must be able to discern who has your best interest at heart and who is trying to slow down your journey. There are people for every situation of life. There are people who want to see you succeed. There are people who want to see you fail. There are people who truly just don't care about you, they just keep you around to see what you can do for them. Having the Holy Spirit and inviting Him into every situation that you come across will allow you to see the time wasted sign or danger sign before you step foot that way.

*When peer pressure compels you to go with the crowd and sin-
ners invite you to join in, you must simply say "NO!" When
the gang says – "We're going to steal an kill and get away
with it. We'll take down the rich and rob them. We'll swal-
low them up alive and take what we want from whomever
we want. Then we'll take their treasures and fill our homes
with loot. So come on and join us. Take your chance with us.
We'll divide up all we get; we'll each end up with big bags
of cash!" – my son, refuse to go with them and stay far away
from them. 16 For crime is their way of life and bloodshed
their specialty. To be aware of their snare is the best way of
escape. They'll resort to murder to steal their victims' assets,
but eventually it will be their own lives that are ambushed.
In their ungodly disrespect for God, they bring destruction
on their own lives.* (Proverbs 1:10-19 TPT)

It doesn't matter the situation. Death has many forms, and it doesn't
always have to be physical or in the grave. There is death of mindset,
death of dreams and goals, death in relationships, and death in
finances. All of these can occur if you keep bad company around you
and entertain those who continue to digress and are okay with it.

PROGRESSIVE POTENTIAL

We will go back to the saying, "You have so much potential!" This is
a saying I have heard my entire life. Mainly on the basketball court
but still have heard it a lot. I molded my identity into basketball and
being just a ball player. My mother and father would always tell me,
"You are a man of God first and then a basketball player." Let's just
say this, if basketball wasn't attached to my name, then you were
wrong about me and didn't know me. I could not see myself as anything else. Although I know how to play the saxophone, although

I love to write poetry, although I love to cook, although I love to edit videos, although I love to travel, although I have the desire to be a husband and father one day, although I love to teach and encourage people, have you had enough, and do you get the point?

God has truly blessed me with more than just basketball. I always thought basketball would be the end to be all. I play the game, I make the money, and my name is in headlights. Not once did I look at basketball to enhance everything else God blessed me with. I didn't look at the fact that I do love to help people out and that basketball could be a tool that could allow me to help people out. Maybe the dreams my future wife has could be obtained because of my love for basketball. That my kids would be set for life because of my love for basketball. My thought process was too small and in return, I looked at God too small.

So, what if I never played an NBA game or a game of basketball again? I never thought that way because I "had to make it." My trust and reliance were in myself, not the God who gave me life. Sidenote. We cannot do anything on our own strength and ego! Grinding can be a hamster wheel. You are exhausting yourself, slaving to get to a goal! Here is the thing I want you to realize; when you are destined to get to your goal, you have got to rest, and you have got to pace yourself. No matter the situation, you must pace yourself. You cannot reach your full potential being tired. Well, Azlan, time waits for no one! Yes, you are correct, and since we all have the same amount of time every day, I am going to rest up and have fresh ideas and a fresh mind, while you grind on the same mindset that has kept you stagnant.

Ladies and Gents, do you realize how much prosperity is in rest. God doesn't want you exhausted and useless. He wants you fresh and renewed, daily! God's yoke is easy, and His burden is light, so rest in Him and allow the Holy Spirit to guide you and show you what to work on and how to work on it. Many times, we get so impatient and are in such a hustle to find a sign from God. Some of the moments when I was most worried is when God just wanted me to rest and take it easy. God is always speaking, but are we listening? God is always speaking but are we talking and worried while He's trying to give you an answer? God is always speaking but when He gives you an answer, are you obedient?

Potential is fulfilled when you're obedient. Who or what are you being obedient to? Are you being obedient to that job that makes you want to cuss everyone and their dog out? Are you being obedient to the relationship that hasn't progressed in years? Are you being obedient to your own desires and flesh? Or are you being obedient to God and His word? One thing I have noticed is that when God has told me to do something and I don't question it, the result has turned out better than what I thought it would.

The truth is that there are some things God needs to get out of you that you cannot do in a relationship with someone else. There are things that God needs to put in you that nobody else can while you're in your single season. I know for a fact that while writing this book, God is trying to show me things that not only will help whoever is reading this book but help me out as well. I know that when I am supposed to court my future wife, that I am going to need to spend a lot of time with her to learn her. I know that God has things that He has to get out of me before I enter that season. In fulfilling the potential that you have in other areas, at that point what you're also fulfilling is purpose. There is much potential in purpose.

If God tells you to pick up and move to a different state because He needs you there, what would you do? (That's what He told me by the way). I made a promise to the Lord that in 2021, that I would just be obedient to whatever He told me to do for Him. I didn't want to necessarily focus on my own goals, I just wanted to build up the heart and trust in me to do whatever He says. In doing that, the potential that I've always possessed is now manifesting itself in more ways than just one, basketball.

I encourage you to ask the Lord today, what is it that you need me to do for you? Truth is, we have asked this question over and over. And many of us probably have many unanswered questions from God because we didn't do what He told us to do 5 years ago. This is where we become stagnant because we saw another opportunity that we may like instead of accepting the opportunity that God had provided for us way back. When you figure out your why, when you figure out what potential you have and which potentials you have surrounded yourself with, truly ask God to show you and He will.

You must be able to discern who has your best interest at heart and who is trying to slow down your journey.

The book that God told you to write 5 years ago, and you started it and never finished it, finish it. The business God put on your heart to start, finish it. The schooling you started but felt like you weren't good enough, finish it. We cannot do it on our own, but we can do it better with the help of the Holy Spirit. Find out your why and don't let the potential aka the calling on your life that God has for you to be digressive. Don't let the great ideas and the rich wisdom you have on the inside of you become stagnant. Press through and allow God to guide you and be progressive in your potential which allows you to walk in your purpose. In the next chapter we will continue to talk about the stagnant stage with being in love with idea of purpose as opposed to preparing for your destiny! Stop daydreaming!

3

BEING IN LOVE WITH THE IDEA

I REMEMBER WATCHING MY FAVORITE TV show, Martin. I remember the episode when Martin and Gina escaped from their family to get married on a beach. They had just the maid of honor and the best man. Cole was supposed to be there, but he got on the wrong plane. The wedding was simple and small, but it got the job done, and at the end of the day Martin and Gina were happy. It didn't matter what anybody else thought, they did what they wanted to do. Prior to escaping away, all of Martin's family showed up, and Gina's parents showed up. There was major clashing and disagreements that happened, and Martin and Gina just couldn't take it anymore. They both had an idea of what their wedding would be like, but at the end of the day, it was completely different than what they both had the idea about. How many times have we gotten into a situation, and it turned out completely different than what you thought it would be? I can raise both hands on that question.

See, I saw myself being married young. I saw myself married at like 23, having kids by 25, and being in the NBA "living my best life!" Let's fast forward. I am 28, single as a pringle, not in the NBA, yet, and guess what I am still living my best life. What I failed to realize is the work it takes to be in a relationship, and that's just the relationship. We won't even bring up marriage yet. I was always looking forward to marriage and the excitement of it, but I was skipping the most important part which was the single stage. I was so in love with the idea of marriage and being with someone, that I had completely forgotten that I had to learn how to be on my own. Majority of my life I have been "single", but I had not been alone. My title or relationship status is single, but my heart was scattered.

SINGLE BUT NOT ALONE

The term single has many different open doors attached to it. Society and lots of other people say live your life, you're single, you can do whatever you want, enjoy your singleness. The question I want to ask you is in your single season, what are you doing in it? For someone who has been single majority of their life, I really had to sit down and think about this question. Majority of my single season was daydreaming about my marriage season. I would think about who I might marry, how am I going to propose, how big the wedding will be, who will my kids look like, me or my future wife? So many fantasies for someone who doesn't even know what they will be eating for dinner that night. When I would meet someone, those daydreams and fantasies would come out first because guess what, that's what I would mainly be thinking about. This would be a greater thought than basketball for me.

I would see my grandparents, and I would see how much they loved each other, and all the trips they would take across the world, and how my grandpa made sure my grandma was taken care of. When you have a good example of relationship, of course you might want what they have, however you don't want to have to walk in the same shoes they did to get to where they got to. My grandpa would say that all the time. When a young man would come up to him and say "Mr. Calloway, I want to be like you when I grow up. I want to love my wife the way you do, I want to be a good father like you, I just want to be like you." My grandpa, a man of great wisdom, would simply say, "You might want to be like me, but you don't want to take the journey that I had to take to get here."

One thing that has changed the world as we know it is social media. I will touch on this a few times throughout this book because it is necessary that we explain the effect of it. It's so easy to see someone's relationship flourishing on social media and think you want what they have. Ladies and gents, that stuff takes major work. Not necessarily the work that you put into the relationship when you're in one, but the work you put in when you weren't in one. When you are single, what are you doing? Are you just dating around because you're single and don't have to answer to anybody? You're in control of everything so you keep people to a distance just in case something goes wrong or just in case a situation seems like what you have already dealt with in the past. A lot of people call it being guarded and careful, but in some instances, it's treating one off your past. Sometimes, you will treat one off their own past based on the conversation you all have had.

Take it from someone who has been treated off both, my past and the others past, it is not good, and it hurts. It really hurts when you are really trying to be better and listening to God, and the other person doesn't see it or feel it. This is another reason why you must be submitted to the Holy Spirit. He will show you what to share and speak about with people and what not to. But guess what, I am single, and I can do whatever I want to. When you're someone who wears their heart on their sleeve, like I have in the past, dating casually and having options is not a good idea. I thought I would want to have many options of women because if one situation failed, I had a backup plan.

This is me being honest and y'all don't be fake and act like some of y'all haven't done that or thought that way. However, if you haven't thought that way, congrats and great respect to you. The point I am making here is, in seasons where I would date, what I was doing in that mindset was creating a wedge in my heart to say, one person isn't good enough. Another thing I was doing was telling God that I don't trust Him because I keep doing it my way. I thought being single meant I was lonely, and that was not the case. I thought I had to suffer for all the things that I did out of order, and it was punishment for that. One thing dating casually taught me, was I had formed a habit of practicing how not to be content and satisfied in a marriage and ultimately was practicing how to be unfaithful and dissatisfied.

There is a major difference of being lonely and being alone. A lot of times we put ourselves in a lonely state of mind. Sometimes we make ourselves be alone. Lonely is literally having nobody to talk to, rely on, be around, and nobody is texting you back or answering your phone calls. But if God is always with us, are we truly ever lonely? I remember I kept saying I was lonely because I didn't have a girlfriend. However, I played basketball every day, I had my mom and dad, I had my dog Tabasco, and I was at school with a bunch of people! The problem wasn't that I was lonely, the problem was I felt alone in an area where I wanted to be joined with someone in the romantic arena. The truth is I have never been lonely. I just had a strong desire to be seen with someone and it be a good time and hopefully one day we would be married.

I mean here I am single majority of my life and truth is, I am a good guy. I am not perfect, and I allowed my flesh to get in the way of a lot of good girls and good situations. Even the ones who did say yes to me and gave me a chance, it didn't work! The enemy will always be right there to put thoughts in your head. He will say you are not good enough; he will say that you did all you could, and it still didn't work, he will tell you that nobody will ever love you. The enemy will do all of this and say all of this when you are single. But again, you are not alone.

The enemy will always try to find something to say or someone to attack, its literally his job. The enemy comes to kill, steal, and destroy. Therefore, it's so important to build your relationship with the Lord for yourself and not rely on a church building to do so. I do believe it's important to go to church but what happens when the enemy is right there at the foot of your bed at 3 am whispering sweet and dangerous nothings to you? The church isn't open, and nobody is awake. We must call on God and stay in His presence.

No matter where you are in your life, you are not alone. The journey may feel lonely, but you are not alone. Holy Spirit is and always has been right there to show you what God needs you to do in this time of life. One thing I have

> **We must call on God and stay in His presence.**

learned is there are certain things God needs you to learn and do while you're single. There is a certain level of focus you must have to complete the things that God needs you to do. Doesn't matter what the task is, when you are by yourself you are more likely to get the task done instead of focusing on someone else who might be relying on you to "complete them," as Tom Cruise said. If someone is pulling you away from God as opposed to pushing you toward Him, that's a red flag. They may look good, and Jesus might come out their mouths here and there, but at the end of the day, it won't matter how good the person is if you aren't where you need to be and doing what God needs you to do.

SCROLLING

In the last chapter, we discussed stagnant potential. One of the most dangerous things you can do today is scrolling. Now back in the day they might have called it trolling, but today scrolling is used to waste time on social media. You swipe up and up and up, no Cardi B, to see what other people are doing. You see what the word on the street is, no Martin, and you see what gossip or rumors might be swirling around. You see what girl or boy is doing what. You see which fine girls you can add today. You see who's dm's you can hop into. You see who has sexual content… I mean oops did I take it a little too far? We have become so interested—and some of us infatuated—with what other people are doing. And, in the process our opportunities and goals are being put to the side.

I remember my days of being addicted to pornography, and how I thought I would be only watching for a few minutes. After watching a video, I would look up and two hours had passed. I was wasting time and damaging my mind at the same time. More importantly I spent two hours pulling myself away from God when I could've spent two hours getting closer to God. Even if those two hours weren't being directed toward God, I could've put those two hours toward basketball. I spent two hours indulging in something that would never be able to fulfill me. I

> *There is a certain level of focus you must have to complete the things that God needs you to do.*

could've put those two hours toward something that would eventually be able to take care of my family and friends for the rest of mine and their lives.

Time is something we can't get back. When I think of all the times I watched porn, let's just say I don't want to even imagine the countless, wasteful hours that I spent watching something trying to get a fill of something that would leave me emptier than before. I hear people say all the time, "Well if I watch porn, at least I'm not having sex with anyone." Let me put you on game real quick. Do you not know sex is meant to be more of a mental connection and a spiritual connection than just a physical connection? If you are constantly filling your head with women or men having sex, you disconnect your mind from reality. It has been said countless times that watching porn is no different than doing heroine. The same area of your brain that needs that fix of drugs is the same area that needs the fix of sex. Indulging your mind in something that is not real pulls you away from reality.

LET'S JUST BE REAL

No matter how much you think pornography is helping you, it is pulling you away from God—more away from reality and real life. I heard that addiction to porn is one of the number one causes of erectile dysfunction in men. It makes sense! When you make those connections with the computer screen and not an actual woman, why would you be turned on by a real woman? Also, why would the woman God provided for you to be your wife turn you on when you are looking at so many different women? I am speaking to the gentlemen here in this section. Women cannot compete with that, at all! Men, we get into these perverted fetishes when it comes to porn. When you are trying to make love to your wife, all the sudden you feel like your wife is not good enough or will not be good enough for you in the bedroom because you're expecting all these freaky things to go down that she is not supposed to do.

Men, we have got to understand that we are created to be the priest, providers, and protectors of our home. Now men, I also know that when it comes to sex, it's important to us. Sex is a beautiful thing because God created it. However, sex has been molded into a perverted way to "embrace your independence." If nobody knows or sees our thoughts, it's okay right?

> *Keep your thoughts continually fixed on all that is authentic and real, honorable and admirable, beautiful and respectful, pure and holy, merciful and kind. And fasten your thoughts on every glorious work of God, praising Him always.*
>
> (Philippians 4:8 TPT)

Well, how do I keep my thoughts pure and holy, Azlan? Like I truly want to be free of thinking lustfully but it's just so hard. Well friends, I am here to give you hope and let you know that you can be set free. I know how hard it can be to not have lustful thoughts, especially when you used to be addicted to porn and lust. It can be hard when society is shoving sex and lust down your throat and trying to blind you with lust blinders. Let me be the first to say, because you struggle with these things does not mean that God loves you any less. He will be disappointed, but just like any good father, He still loves you despite what you've done.

> Just like any good father, He still loves you despite what you've done.

The enemy wants to get you to believe that because of what you've done, you can't be free and that you are a terrible person. Lies, lies, and more lies! One of the reasons a lot of us can't move forward is because of the lies we have believed. Seeds of doubt, pain, insecurity, and low self-esteem were planted in your mind; you let it grow and fester. The one thing someone told you that hurt tremendously, spread like cancer in your mind and you ended up believing it.

I learned that you have the option to think about what you're thinking about. Once those negative thoughts come up, stop thinking about it. You may ask, well how do you do that? Just try it. When a thought comes up, try your hardest to switch up the thought you have and replace it with something better. Think about the good things God has done for you. Think about the places God has brought you from. Think about your good memories and just simply ask God to show you how to get rid of the thoughts that torment your mind.

I believe that Paul said it best.

> *We can demolish every deceptive fantasy that opposes God and break through every arrogant attitude that is raised up in defiance of the true knowledge of God. We capture, like prisoners of war, every thought and insist that it bow in obedience to the Anointed One.* (2 Corinthians 10:5 TPT)

So, you see ladies and gents, we should take those thoughts that try to oppose what God says and take them captive and put them in the cell of "forget that mess". That cell that you put those thoughts into is the love and care of our Heavenly Father. The cross that Jesus died on, you put all negativity on that. The Lord wants all our sins, thoughts, mistakes, failures, false ideas of what is good for us, He wants it all. When it comes to "falling in love with the idea," some of us have fallen into the love of the idea of not being the best we can be.

SINGLED OUT FOR PREPARATION

We have believed the lie. Nobody will ever be able to love me because of what I've been through. I am not qualified for that job. I am too skinny to play in the NBA. I know God loves me and has redeemed me, but I used to act like a whore, and I feel used up. I don't think anybody would want me or know my true value. I have multiple kids, who would want that? All these thoughts are what you must take captive and allow God to work what only He can do. There is one word that covers all the things that have held us back. That word is Purity!

THE COVERING OF PURITY

When we think of the word purity, we tend to immediately go to the thought of someone being a virgin and inexperienced. I always would hear that God could make you pure again if you asked Him to. For me, that was hard to accept. I mean I had been in church. I had been respectful to people. I was polite. I was a hard worker. That's what people on the outside saw. However, there was a whole different side that people didn't see that had attached itself to me and I allowed it to happen. When coming into the light, dark things come out too and my darkness felt overbearing. I could've said, well, at least what I did wasn't as bad as homie over there. What has comparison ever done for anyone? All comparison does is take the responsibility off you. Ultimately, it is a fear tactic to protect yourself from the truth.

When you accept the truth and then give it to the Lord, that purity that you never thought you could grasp soon becomes in your heart and God uses it to bring glory to His kingdom. I remember having a conversation with a friend, and she explained what purity meant to her. If there was a person who defined purity in my eyes, it was her. She explained that when people think of purity, they automatically think it's a sex thing, but it's really a heart thing. She said you can have someone who has never had sex, but their heart is far from being pure. Not only do you pursue a pure heart, but you pursue pure thoughts. You pursue pure conversations. You guard your eyes and your ears. You purify those toxic thoughts and people that are around you. She said purity isn't a season, it's a lifestyle.

You don't just choose purity for a season to get married or to just say, "I tried". You live out purity no matter where you are. In your job, on the basketball court, when you're home alone, in your friendships and relationships. No matter where you are, you don't try purity, but you choose purity. Time for another definition!

Purity is the condition or quality of being pure; freedom from anything that debases, contaminates, or pollutes.

Jesus is the ultimate purifier. Anything in your life that has been contaminated or polluted must be conditioned into freedom. Purity is offered daily, and it is something that is needed to be the best you can be every single day.

When you are falling in love with ideas, make sure they are positive and honoring the Lord our God. He wants your dreams and goals to be successful and fulfilled. You must ask yourself, what ideas have I fallen in love with? Were these ideas positive or negative? Were they pure or polluted? Did I invite God into anything I was thinking or was I just doing it alone by choice? Regardless of what you have done or not done, God loves you. He wants you to be able to fall in love with His ideas and His direction for your life. I promise you will not regret it and it will change your life forever! In this next chapter, we will go over how the things that happened in your past can affect your future if you choose to allow the negative past things to control your future!

4

THE PAST THAT COULD AFFECT MY FUTURE

> *Immediately they dropped their nets and left everything and behind and followed Jesus.* (Matthew 4:20 TPT)

T HIS SOUNDS EASY TO do right? Just drop everything you have built, worked for, and invested into and just follow someone. Imagine someone coming along and just saying, "Follow me". At first, you would just be like who are you and why would I follow you? A lot of times, we need to see the proof in the pudding. We need cause to do something or take a leap of faith. Is it really faith if you already have the evidence though?

> *For we live by faith, not by what we see with our eyes.*
> (2 Corinthians 5:7 TPT)

SINGLED OUT FOR PREPARATION

You see many times; I have acted upon what has happened and what I have seen happen in my life or other people's experiences. I made decisions or lived my life based off the evidence. A situation would happen, and I would say to myself, I will never go through that again. I remember when I would start working out and I would be super sore and could barely walk, and I would say I won't do this again. I remember being hurt in a situation and saying I would never let that person hurt me again. Again, I remember when I was deep into watching porn and I would repent repeatedly. I ate escargot and I said I would never do that again, and yeah, I will never do that again. The prior situations though, I did repeatedly. It was a rough time getting out of those pits.

As I stated earlier, my dad would say boy you are hardheaded and yes, I was. I was raised based on forgiveness and so I knew I had to forgive. I didn't have to forgive for the other person, but I had to forgive for me and my well-being. The problem with my type of forgiveness is that I would forgive but felt like I had to let the person back in my life. I speak on forgiveness toward humans because at the end of the day, that is where forgiveness needs to happen. You can be mad at your basketball for being flat or for popping but your basketball doesn't have a soul. Your basketball didn't call you out of your name or do damage to your character. People cause you to have to forgive. I can't tell you how many times I let people back in my life that caused hurt and confusion. My mom always would tell me that just because you forgive someone doesn't mean that they must be a part of your life.

Just because you forgive someone doesn't mean that they must be a part of your life.

For the longest time, I thought me having a big heart was a problem. Things in the past that kept happening repeatedly really had me wanting to be this ruthless, careless person who just wanted to be selfish. I was tired of being used, told I wasn't good enough, and just doubting me period. What I should've been tired of was listening to the lies of the enemy. I should've been tired of believing everything that people said instead of believing the things that God said about me. What I was doing was allowing the things of the past to affect my future.

TRIPPING FORWARD

Have you ever heard the saying you can't move forward while look-ing back? Well, that saying is very true. I know many times I have tried to move forward in life but couldn't let go of what was already behind. I found myself being one of the old heads in the barbershop talking about all the good things I did in high school basketball or what girls I used to talk to. I remember being in the barbershop listening to those guys and just laughing at them because they couldn't move on. Being young, I didn't know what those guys had experienced in life as to why they didn't get to where they dreamed to be. I just knew that when I got to that age, I wouldn't be that guy. Well, I became that guy for a moment in life at a young age. I felt that what was in the past would make me feel better if I talked and bragged about. How far from the truth was I?

Now as I have stated multiple times in this book already, I have the dream and the desire to get to the NBA. Holding on to the past won't get you to where you want to be in the future. It's like being a track runner and competing to win the race. When you watched Usain Bolt race, did you ever see him turn around to see who was behind him? You might have seen him peek to the side to see if anyone was near him, but you never saw his head turn to see who was next to him or behind him.

If you aren't picking up on what I am putting down, then let me explain. In this race of life, we don't aim to run backwards. While running our individual race, we cannot turn around to see who or what is behind us. I remember a time when I was younger, and my teammates and I had a memorable race. The fastest kid took off and was ahead by a decent length and when he thought he was about to win, he turned around to see his sweet victory and then ran dead smack into a car. As he fell to the ground, we all laughed as we ran past him because he thought he had the victory. Now, although it was funny to us, best believe that teammate was in pain. I mean imagine you running full speed into a ton of steel. Although he was in physical pain, he also was embarrassed. Us laughing at him hysterically didn't help either.

I have seen people running who turned their head and got off focus and either lost the race or tripped and fell. Since I talked about one of my teammates, I think it's time to tell my not paying attention story. I was playing football in the yard and playing catch. As I took off to run my route, I was focused and ready to receive the ball. As I ran the route and turned back to look for the ball, all I remember was hitting something extremely hard and flying back. So, my friend ran into a car, and I ran into a brick house. Now let me explain the emotions I felt in the moment.

1. I was mad because I ran into a house. I mean like how did I not see a whole house right in front of me?
2. I was in excruciating pain and couldn't move my arm and I was crying.
3. How did the person who threw the ball, the person who was guiding me, not say watch out for the house?

I mean they had me looking like George of the Jungle or Martin in the episode when he fought Tommy Hearns. That brings me to the next point of this chapter, who or what is guiding you? Who or what is your GPS?

GPS (GOD PROVIDES STEPS)

Speaking of George of the Jungle, there was a moment where I had a reenactment of him running into a tree. My mom was trying to teach me how to ride a bike without training wheels. She guided me and eventually let go. I was doing great for about 5 seconds until I panicked and as the situation got wobbly, there was a nice big tree there waiting to embrace me. As the bike stopped and me not riding it anymore, I found myself face to face with the tree. Bark does not taste good, and I was scratched up and embarrassed. To make things worse for me, my mom was rolling laughing. Like this lady is supposed to be comforting me, not laughing in my face. However, my mom has always been tough on me. Love ya mommy! (Inside Joke). The part I didn't mention was I had stopped listening to my mom when things got wobbly and focused on the situation as opposed to the one who was guiding me.

As she was trying to guide me, I steered off the path and thought I could do it on my own. Think of a time or times that you steered off the path of life because you thought you had everything under control. Think of a time when you thought you had something in the bag, or it was guaranteed, and pride set in. You wanted to see how much you accomplished and ended up running into the steel car of life. Or even better, think of a time you were on a route, and you ran the correct route, you did what was needed and when you turned to receive your reward, you run into a brick house of life because of who you allowed to guide you and the instruction you followed.

We see this example clearly when Jesus was walking on the water and He invited Peter to join him.

> *Peter shouted out, "Lord, if it's really you, then have me join you on the water!" "Come and join me," Jesus replied. So Peter stepped out onto the water and began to walk toward Jesus. But when he realized how high the waves were, he became frightened and started to sink. "Save me, Lord!" he cried out. Jesus immediately stretched out his hand and lifted him up and said, "What little faith you have! Why would you let doubt win?" And the very moment they both stepped into the boat, the raging wind ceased.* (Matthew 14:28-32 TPT)

You see Peter was already doing the impossible because he did have faith. It's when he noticed what was around him and how the situation seemed bigger than his faith is when he began to sink. There is one point in that scripture that really stood out to me. It said when Peter began to sink, immediately, Jesus reached and pulled Peter up when he cried out. The other thing that stood out to me was that as soon as they got in the boat, the wind and storm calmed down. How many times have we let the sight of things overtake the height of our faith? Although Peter was walking on the water, he let the sight of the waves and the wind overtake his faith in something that he was already doing.

This is simply why the bible says to walk by faith and not by sight because what you see can confuse you and put fear into your heart. As soon as Peter took his eyes off Jesus is when he began to sink. I can only imagine that as Peter is sinking, Jesus is telling Peter to stay focused on me and keep your eyes on me. When we take our eyes and focus off the Lord, we can sink, and we can sink fast. Our faith shouldn't be built up in all that is around us and the waves and storms of life. Our faith should be built on the foundation of. If God said it, then it will happen. The thing is, some of us haven't even had the little faith that Peter did because we keep looking back to what has already happened and basing our decisions off past experiences. Some of us have stepped out in faith but then looked around at what others are doing or thinking about the one time you took a risk or a leap of faith and got hurt. We can literally be bound by fear of the past which will affect your future.

> *Trust in the Lord completely, and do not rely on your own opinions. With all your heart rely on Him to guide you, and He will lead you in every decision you make. Become intimate with Him in whatever you do, and He will lead you wherever you go.* (Proverbs 3:5-6 TPT)

As you see, God will guide you, every step of the way. In building your relationship with God, He makes the decisions and answers to your prayers clear as well. As the scripture says, become intimate with God so He can guide you.

When Jesus left the earth, He said that He will send us the helper. The Helper is the Holy Spirit! The same spirit that led Jesus and guided Him, lives in us if we ask to receive Him. Allow the Holy Spirit to be your GPS. I know that I wouldn't really know where to go

We can literally be bound by fear of the past which will affect your future.

or how to get to certain places if I did not have GPS. It's the same in life when you receive the Holy Spirit. He guides you each step of the way in every aspect of life. Not just jobs but relationships, dreams and goals, thoughts and lifestyle.

DESIRING TO RETURN TO EGYPT

I want to really emphasize the dangers of wanting to turn around or wanting to cling to the past. I just love the bible so much because there are so many stories that are relatable and helpful. The story I am about to talk about is the story of Moses and the Israelites. God sent Moses to get His people out of Egypt and set them free. God promised a land flowing with milk and honey and a land of prosperity. In Egypt, the Israelites were slaves and had been for years. Once the slaves were freed and were headed to the promise land, they hit a bump in the road and got discouraged and impatient.

The crowds became restless and began to question if God really brought them out and if the promise land was even a thing.

> *Their voices rose in a great chorus of protest against Moses and Aaron. "If only we had died in Egypt, or even here in the wilderness!" they complained. "Why is the Lord taking us to this country only to have us die in battle? Our wives and our little ones will be carried off as plunder! Wouldn't it be better for us to return to Egypt?" Then they plotted among themselves, "Let's choose a new leader and go back to Egypt!"*
> (Numbers 14:2-4 NLT)

One thing we must understand is that when the Lord says He is going to do something, He is going to do it. You might be wondering like hold up, didn't God part the sea for the Israelites to escape the Egyptian army? The answer is yes. However, that happened before they began to question if this thing was real and plot to have a new leader. So, you saw God part the sea for you and made an escape out of no way, and you still are having doubts. We aren't done yet. Before the people began complaining, Moses sent some scouts to check on the promised land.

After exploring the land for forty days, the men returned, to Moses, Aaron, and the whole community of Israel at Kadesh in the wilderness of Paran. They reported to the whole community what they had seen and showed them the fruit they had taken from the land. This was their report to Moses: "We entered the land you sent us to explore, and it is indeed a bountiful country – a land flowing with milk and honey. Here is the kind of fruit it produces. But the people living there are powerful, and their towns are large and fortified. We even saw giants there, the descendants of Anak!

(Numbers 13:25-28 NLT)

Again, the Israelites had the evidence they needed to know that God was correct and what He promised them actually existed. How many of us have seen the evidence happen for someone else but because it didn't happen to us, it put a dent in our faith? There were countless times in my life when I saw miracles happen to everyone around me. I was genuinely happy but in the back of my mind I was always thinking, when would this happen to me? I mean I would even see people who didn't believe in God get blessed beyond their wildest dreams. They would just thank any and everybody but God. I would sit there and think to myself, in the words of Haha Davis, "THIS IS BEYOND ME!"

Let me say that God can use anybody to bring glory to His kingdom. No matter where they are at the time, or no matter who it is, God can use them. The point I am getting to and why I used the example of the Israelites is because many times we have become impatient. Even when we have seen God move, we still have doubt in our minds. Just because God doesn't move exactly when we want Him to, does not mean that we must go back to what we knew.

49

The Israelites wanted to go back to Egypt because they had developed a comfort in slavery and bondage. Many times, we have molded ourselves to the lifestyle we were used to. So, when God is pulling us out of that place of comfort that is not good for us, it may feel like God is "breaking you." Truth is, God is not breaking you, He is removing you from what you cemented yourself to. Our removal from the mold may look and feel different for all of us. For some of us, all you will have to do is pour water on you to pull you out the mold. For another group of us, it might take a hammer and screwdriver to chip us out of the mold. Then for a good amount of us, like me, it will take a jack hammer and wrecking ball to remove us from the mold.

We have been stuck in the mold of what we think is best for so long, we develop comfort, and we develop habit. I know that you can get stuck at a job for a long time because you put in the work, you put in the time, and it is convenient for your lifestyle. I know with some people; they have not only been stuck in their own mold but other people's mold as well. Therefore, when someone breaks up, they have to find who they are again. They became so focused on pleasing the other, they lost who they were. Through it all, whether water or wrecking ball, if you trust in our Lord and rely on the Holy Spirit to guide you, you will be set free and able to move forward. You will not have to go back to Egypt and suffer!

HOW BAD DO YOU WANT IT?

I know being on the court, everybody wants to win. Now, everybody may want to win but have you prepared yourself to win? Have you worked out hard enough to last and play through the entire game? Have you worked hard enough in the weight room to be strong and be able to stand your ground? Are you mentally tough enough to bounce back when you make a mistake? Although you aren't hitting your shots, are you being valuable in other areas of the game? These are all questions you can ask yourself in life too. Anybody can go to the rec and just shoot around and hope that you win the game. But it takes special people to prepare for the moments to win in games and be in the position to win. Are you preparing when nobody is around or watching?

Many of us say we want to be married but are in love with the idea as opposed to the preparation. Are you wanting to be married but practicing unfaithful tendencies? You can say that you want to be married but haven't been delivered from your porn addiction and can't keep your eyes off every piece of flesh that walks by. Just because you get married does not mean that everything will be like a Houdini magic trick. If you have not healed from those lustful ways of acting and thinking, you will carry those habits and mindset into your future marriage. Use the single season to work on those things so that when you do get married things will be easier than having to go back to Egypt, and then trying to get re-free.

If you have been stuck in a job for years, and you feel content, but nothing has changed and no progression has been made, pray and ask God for clarity and what you should do. Now again, if you want to stay in the same place, that is on you. I truly believe God always wants us to progress in every aspect of our lives.

I always say, our blessings are right outside of our comfort zones and miracles outside our lazy bed. Sometimes ladies and gents, we have got to step outside and take a risk. That is what faith really is. Now if God tells you not to move, then don't move! Too many times we do things and ask God to bless it and He never said to move. If God places something on your heart and it is really pulling on you, seek God. Ask Him to show you how to go about it. Just always be submitted to the Holy Spirit and I promise you that He will never lead you down a path of failure. It may not be easy, but it will be worth it. Just. Trust. Him!

5

HEALING IN THE HEALER

T HERE ARE MANY COPING mechanisms but there is only one healer. Throughout time, many people try to cope with trauma and pain and hurt with things that will hurt them more. A few of my coping mechanisms were basketball, eating, and lust. I would write poetry from time to time but good gracious they were depressing. Basketball was always something I knew I could go to when I needed to clear my mind. The night my father passed; I was up till 3 in the morning just shooting around outside my dorm. When I wanted to get away, I would just pick up my ball and it would be me, the hoop, and God. Now, I wouldn't necessarily say eating was a coping mechanism, your boy just loves to eat and eat good. The lust, yeah, a big-time coping mechanism.

When I was in middle school, I felt like I was the most rejected dude I have ever heard of or known. I didn't realize how deep that cut until I experienced real trauma in my life. When my father passed, the girls in school wanted to "comfort" me and so what do you think I did; that's right I let them do just that. Being a man, I knew which girls would comfort me and go a little bit above and beyond, if you know what I mean. In the unstable mindset I was in, l thought that would comfort me and take the pain away a little, but it put me in a worse mindset and not only hurt me but the other as well. At the end of the day, everyone involved in the situation was being used, except God!

We all have our different things we struggle with, and we all have our different things we use to cope with stress, trauma, problems. Some people drink, some smoke, some have sex, some spend money, A LOT of us cope on Facebook or twitter, whatever it is, at some point we all have used something to cope with. But what happens when all our coping mechanisms are surrounded around God and the word? What if I coped with the scriptures? What if I coped with prayer? What if I coped with worship? I won't say that the pain won't be real, but the healing process is better and you're actually healing, not harming. We can become selfish in our misery. When people aren't feeling bad for us, or liking our pictures on Instagram, we become sad and even bitter. We will talk more about that in the next chapter, but for now we must grasp where our real healing comes from and how we go about it.

SINGLE SEASON BUCKET LIST

Having a conversation with a friend, she was telling me how the best thing she could've done in her single season was create a single season bucket list. She created a list and made sure that she did everything on the list and wouldn't think about dating until she finished everything on the list. While accomplishing her goals, she was able to really learn what she liked to do and learn new things about herself. The one thing that stood out to me about what she said was how she didn't need anybody to do what she liked to do.

One of the false narratives I believe that are created in the dating world is that you must be with someone to truly enjoy life. I know there are things that will be more fun when you can enjoy them with your significant other, but you do not NEED someone to enjoy things. I used to watch my parents and grandparents, and there were things that the men wanted to do that the ladies didn't. There were things that the ladies wanted to do that the men didn't. However, there were many things they enjoyed doing together and that is why they were a couple. So, do not hold up your life waiting on someone to do the things you truly want to do. Healing also comes when you are dedicated to just you and God in the single season.

Being single doesn't mean you can't talk to anybody or go out and have fun, unless God told you not to. Take the time to really work on those things that you need to work on. Build that business that you have wanted to build. Get that body that you always dreamed of. (I am on the swole body marathon as we speak). The single season is the most important time of your life. It is not about preparing just for marriage, but your career, your family and kids, your friends, and overall, just your purpose. It is hard to fulfill purpose when you are not healed.

There are times when you may feel like you will never heal but God will always bring you into a situation or surround you with people who can bring healing. So, if you are not whole, that's okay because God knows what is best and even if you can't see it, God can and will bring that healing to you. Yes, God can heal through people.

I remember a time in my life when I was straddling the fence. I was doing the church thing and my own lust thing. I was down in Tuskegee and my friends and I went to a place called The Coop. They had some of the best chicken wings I ever had. As we were leaving, one of the guys outside the place stopped us. You could tell life had dealt him a hard card and you could tell he had done some drugs. I remember him touching each of our hands and all my other friend's hands were warm. He touched mine and one hand was warm, and the other was cold because I was holding a pop. It was almost as if he snapped out of his state and as clear as day just looked at me and said, "Son, you can't be lukewarm. You know the word says not to be lukewarm or God will spew you out." As soon as he finished, he went back to the state he was in prior to the knowledge he just slapped me with. Although my friends didn't know what was going on, I knew exactly what happened and what he was referring to.

We cannot be lukewarm and living on both sides of the fence. It is so dangerous and so critical to life and those around us. At that point, I knew I couldn't live two lives and I would have to decide on who I was going to follow: myself or God. Living lukewarm is just like living two lifestyles. You just pray that nobody finds out the dark side of your life. I think about people who have experienced church hurt and how that type of hurt is real. People have been hurt by other people in the church, pastors, deacons, etc. One thing that we must realize when it comes to church is that we are all human. Yes, there are trustworthy pastors and church folk that exist. There are also dirty, perverted, and confused church folk as well.

One thing we must realize is that all of us have a past and have grown up experiencing something. We don't know what a person who caused us hurt went through themselves. Does it justify or even make the pain better, absolutely not! However, therefore we must trust in God and not put our trust in just people. Some of you may say, well Azlan, I have put my trust in God, and I still ended up hurt. I will tread lightly when I say this, but before when I mentioned about making decisions first and then inviting God in and saying you will trust in Him, we must ask God about everything. In finding a church home, you must ask God is that where you're supposed to be. Many people have been fooled by the hype of the church and not reeled in by the spirit. Truth is, there are many churches that are driving their congregations away from God instead of to Him. If you are not in tune with the Holy Spirit, you can easily be drawn into a cult.

Now let's switch gears really quick. There are a lot of women and men who go to church to find their mate. They really aren't there for the Lord, but simply there to find someone in what many would consider, the right place. Growing up, this is one of the oldest tricks in the book but for some reason many continue to fall for it. Now I am not saying that you shouldn't find your wife or husband in the church, technically, that's where you want to find them.

Ladies, if a man approaches you at the church and shows interest in you but can't tell you what his favorite part of the sermon was, that might mean he was only there on assignment, and that assignment being to get you off course because of his selfish needs. Again, not all men are like that! Still ladies, you cannot be fooled by the creased suit, compelling cologne, and the fact he says praise the Lord or Hallelujah. You must be submitted to the Holy Spirit and ask is this potential or is it a distraction and a possible fatal attraction.

Men, I will just say this, be submitted to God and the Holy Spirit and He will reveal to you who your wife is. Don't be distracted by the tight dresses and the fact that you see a woman crying in awe of the Lord and you feel that you have to go put your two sense in and comfort her. The Holy Spirit is all the comforter she needs, and you just stay focused on what God is telling you to do and allow Him to show you how to prepare to be the Godly husband that she needs, and that God needs you to be.

BEWARE OF THE "GOD TOLD ME TO TELL YOU"

Part of healing that needs to happen is from people who have spoken into your life that was nowhere near the plan of God. I have seen so many people fall and go away from God because of what someone said to them. They put all their trust in the persons words, and they forgot to ask God if it was meant to be. There have been a couple of occasions where someone had a word of God for me, and it was nowhere near anything that was relevant to my life. I don't want to make it seem like I have always just been so submitted to the Holy Spirit and that I haven't made mistakes because clearly, I have. There have been times where I did hear the Holy Spirit and still chose to do my own thing. But one thing I can say is I do know the voice of the Lord and when He speaks to me. What tends to happen is that when someone gives a false prophecy, we hear the good words and who knows, we might be in a time that hearing those words are needed, but we still must ask God is it so.

> *Many of us are in love with the idea as opposed to the preparation.*

We must not become so desperate to hear good news or a good word to where it can lead us into debt. I'm not just referring to financial debt, but the debt of life, the pit, confusion, hurt, anger and bitterness. Many times, you will see a person who believed so much in something that was prophesied over them, that when it didn't happen, they lost their faith in God. I am saying this to say, don't be that person that always has something to say for God. If God puts it on your heart to tell someone something, talk to them about it. If they say I needed to hear that or that was right on time then say good, and let God do the work. God doesn't really need us to do anything for Him. We choose to follow Him and be obedient or we don't. Don't be the reason why someone turns from God because you thought you heard correctly. Also, if someone comes up to you and says that God told them to tell you something and it's incorrect or you feel off about it, DO NOT allow the seed of false prophecy to form in your mind or heart. You tell the person right then and there that you appreciate trying to encourage me, however, that is not what God is speaking to me right now and keep it moving. When it comes to our lives and our future, it's more than okay to tell someone they were wrong. You don't want anything that is not of God coming near you or growing in you. God knows the desires of your heart and He knows the plans you want to achieve, and He knows that the plans He has for you will come to pass.

> *Keep trusting in the Lord and do what is right in His eyes. Fix your heart on the promises of God, and you will dwell in the land, feasting on his faithfulness. ind delight and true pleasure in Yahweh, and He will give you what you desire the most.* (Psalms 37:3-4 TPT)

> *For I know the plans I have for you," says the Lord. "They are plans for good and not for disaster, to give you a future and a hope.* (Jeremiah 29:11 NLT)

If the plans don't look and sound like that, I don't want it! God has and always will be faithful in every aspect of life. We have to just relax and breathe sometimes. As the scriptures said above, we must fix our hearts on the Lord, that way He can bless us with what we desire most. Sometimes that doesn't look like what we thought it would. But knowing how my God works, He will make it better than what you could've ever thought or seen. God's plan, no Drake, will always be for good and not to destroy but we must be submitted and content in Him.

PARENTAL ADVISORY

We are going to hop into the part that is most important in life and that is forgiveness. We forgive not for the other person but for ourselves. However, I want to name a couple different people groups that you need to forgive in order to move forward and set generational blessings. You ever heard of generational curses? If you have, understand that they are real and they are pivotal. As generations come, we want the next generation to be curse breakers. I was the curse breaker for pornography and sickness in my family line. No longer will that issue be a setback or a slowdown in my family. Although, I forgave my father for having the porn in the house and exposing it to me when I was just looking for Michael Jordan videos, it was not easy.

The hardest part about forgiving my father was I saw how it did damage to his marriage with my mom. Seeing my mom hurt from the addiction, and seeing how she didn't feel good enough, it hurt me to see that. My father was sick and he didn't do as much for himself as I thought he could. It hurt to have to see my mom work extra, take care of him, and raise a teenage boy. I saw my mom do things I have never seen or heard

> *You don't want anything that is not of God coming near you or growing in you.*

of any other spouse do. Not saying they aren't out there; I just don't know. It was hard to see my dad want to get better but ultimately, had little hope. The parts that made it easy for me to forgive him was the support he showed me and the wisdom he would impart to me.

When it came to having support from my parents, I never lacked that one bit. I remember when I had an event for a scholarship I was receiving, literally, my dad tried to escape the nursing home he was in to make it to my event. That's love right there. He wanted to make every single basketball game he could, scholarship event, beautillion event, school project event; if it involved me, my dad would be there. I have friends who never got to experience that. To them, my dad was a father figure to them as well.

So how do you forgive someone who introduced you to what held you back for so long. Well, isn't that what Jesus did for Mary Magdalene, when He told her to go and sin no more after being caught sleeping with a married man? Isn't that what Jesus died for period? He died for those who continue to make mistakes, continue to cause hurt to other people, continue to do what's wrong, continue to cause pain to themselves. Here is the thing; Jesus didn't die because people would accept Him into their lives, He died for a possible yes, not a guaranteed yes.

I looked at the example of Jesus and said to myself, if He could give up His own life for the sake of me being forgiven and giving me another chance, I can forgive my father and whoever else has done harm to me. However, although my dad had the porn in the house, which exposed me, he did not make me watch it. This goes back to what I was saying earlier in the book, it may not be our fault as to why something was introduced to us, but if we make the choice to continue in what we know is not right, then it will be our fault. I knew that watching the porn was not right, even at a young age. Even young, we have the choice, especially if our parents told us not to.

I remember being sick at times and telling my mom that I wasn't feeling well. Her response would be sometimes, "Stop being dramatic." It would cause a scar because I would really be down and out, and she wouldn't realize it until I was passed out somewhere. I'm like man if my mom won't help me, I don't know who

> *Jesus died for a possible yes, not a guaranteed yes.*

will. Maybe Tabasco would help me. But with her reacting that way, from that point on, I would not tell someone if I was sick or not feeling well. The reason my mom would act like that was because when my dad was sick, he was overly dramatic. My mom just thought I had learned patterns and was trying to be like my dad. Now, I did learn some patterns, but I didn't want to be like my dad because I knew the toll it took on me at a young age.

As great as my parents are, still things I had to forgive them for. For many of you, you have experienced way worse things than I ever have. Some of you may not know your parents and feel abandoned. Some may know one parent and not the other. Some may know both parents but never felt loved or accepted. Whatever your situation is with your parents, you must forgive and keep living. I know it's easier said than done, but the one who heals the sick, the one who heals the liar, the one who heals the abandoned, the one who heals the parentless, is the same one who will show you how to forgive your parents. If there is any unforgiveness in your heart toward your parents, I encourage you today to begin the healing process. Allow the Holy Spirit to guide you and show you the exact areas you need healing in. Also, if you're able to, with the guidance of the Lord, if possible, talk with your parents and let them know how certain things affected you and let them know you forgive them. Again, that's only if the Lord tells you to do so.

When you become parents, you don't want your kids to experience the same pain and hurt you did. If you are already parents, take the time you need to work on those things that scarred you. Take the time to go to therapy and let go of the things that make you feel the way you do. Don't allow your kids to suffer because you didn't heal from your suffering. Just because it made you tough does not mean that your kids need to be made tough through the same type of "love" that was shown to you. As I said, we are meant to be generational curse breakers, not generational curse continuers.

HEALED MAN, HEALED MAN, YEAH THAT'S ME

On this last part, we are continuing to talk about forgiveness, but this is the most important level of forgiveness, forgiving yourself. This is the part that many of us skip over at times. We become so focused on forgiving everyone else, which isn't bad, it's necessary, but we forget about ourselves. The reason why we continue to beat ourselves over the head is because we haven't forgiven ourselves. I used to be one who was extremely hard on myself in all aspects of life. We'd lose a game; it was my fault. I didn't pass a test, it was my fault, and yes it was my fault because I didn't study like I should've, but I would begin to think I was stupid.

One thing you must know about me is that I am really competitive. I mean it was a part of my blood from a young light skin. If my little cousin Jacqui was getting more attention than me, I had to make a move. If she was singing a song, I had to try to sing it too. Now, she can actually sing, and I can't and so that's how you know I was trying. My grandpa always beat me in ping pong. He is in heaven now but just wait till I get up there Pop Pop. I laugh because I know he isn't thinking nothing about ping pong.

I talk about me being competitive because just as happy as I am when I win, or how sad I am about losing, I am just as compassionate toward other people and never like to see anybody down or out. There were times when I would pray for someone and have complete confidence that God would work a miracle in their lives, and something worse happened. Now I was not like earlier in the chapter when I said, "God told me to tell you," I would just try to provide some encouragement and back up it up with prayer. However, when the situation would get worse for that person, I would feel terrible. I would beat myself up about what happened and instead of asking that person to forgive me if they felt upset with me, I would put the blame on myself and just internalize it. That my friends is a spirit of pride. Pride against yourself is the worse.

Types of pride against yourself are like saying no to someone who is trying to bless you. When someone is trying to bless you, accept it, especially if you don't have to give it back. When you are so "humble" to not receive a blessing or help, that is prideful. You know you don't have groceries, and someone offers you some groceries and you tell them, "oh no it's fine, I'll be okay, God will provide." Pay attention big head, that is God providing for you. Just because you are upset with yourself for not budgeting correctly or buying that expensive thing you didn't need at the time, does not mean that God won't provide just because you made a mistake. God knows our needs, but you can block your blessings, and other's blessings by trying to be humble but operating in pride. Newsflash, you must keep moving forward.

> *Newsflash: Healing isn't easy, but it's worth it.*

In forgiving yourself, you must acknowledge what you have done. You must acknowledge what you have allowed. You must acknowledge that you have been trying on your own and you have been thinking of God too small. God is a God of grace and mercy. He hears all your prayers; He sees all your struggles and He truly wants to bless you. The thing that keeps us from forgiving ourselves is that we don't want to do the work. We want this miraculous water to just wash everything away and not feel a thing and keep on living. Now God can do that for you but there is a purpose behind the healing. God gets more glory from the work you allow Him to do through you. When has anything been easy in life? Was graduating school easy? Was getting thru a breakup easy? Was applying for that job you weren't qualified for easy? Newsflash: Healing isn't easy, but it's worth it.

Putting in the work in healing will be some of the hardest times you will go through. You have to go back and dig up some painful memories. You have to address the things that you never thought you'd address. You will have to grieve during the process and take the time to do so. We are taught to be strong and to just get through things. We are all in different situations when it comes to grieving. Some of us must be strong for our kids or our family members. In many ways, society teaches us to be strong, not cry, not show emotion, bottle up our emotions and keep moving. Not handling your emotions and letting your emotions control you, will not only affect you, but those around you. Holding in unforgiveness will cause bitterness and unnecessary anger.

I want to continue on the grieving tip for a moment. I think about the "grieving" of my father. I honestly didn't take the time to grieve and didn't feel like I had the time to grieve either. Coming back from Tuskegee, Alabama, I didn't know what to expect. I knew I was happy to be home because I was dealing with losing my father in a place where I knew no one, far from home. But when I got back home, I just had to keep going. I wanted to take some time, but I had to get a job. I wanted to continue to play basketball, so I went to community college to try to gain some credits. The truth is, I was not mentally focused at all. I failed almost all my classes and just was not motivated at all.

In not taking the time to grieve, you can alter a lot of other areas in your life. You can only use motivation for so long before you have to find a different motivation. The help of the Holy Spirit is an everlasting thing, and He will help you through all areas of life, no matter how light or how dark the situation is. There is no pit He can't pull you out of, no pain He can't heal, no torment He can't demolish, and no joy He can't fill. Holy Spirit is God in spirit to help us live this life and live it as it is in heaven. I wish I could put the whole chapter of Romans 8 in here, but I want you to read that yourself. That chapter shows you how to live in the spirit and what the spirit of God does in your life when you ask and accept Him into your life. So, yes, that's your homework. Read Romans 8 and accept the Holy Spirit into your life If you haven't done so already.

To my people who feel like they want to do right, but continue to do wrong and sin, read Romans chapters 6 and 7. I was stuck in that area of life for a long time. Knowing what I was doing was wrong and hurtful but didn't know how to break free from it or why I was even doing it in the first place. That my friends is a hard place to be. You are knowing what's right from wrong but constantly doing what's wrong but not understanding why you're doing it. After reading Romans 6 and 7, it seemed like my life came to life and hadn't been stagnant or dead anymore.

> *And Christ lives within you, so even though your body will die because of sin, the Spirit gives you life because you have been made right with God. The Spirit of God, who raised Jesus from the dead, lives in you. And just as God raised Christ Jesus from the dead, He will give life to your mortal bodies by this same Spirit living within you.*
>
> (Romans 8:10-11 NLT)

So you see, God will renew the parts of your life that feel dead and useless. He will give you the strength to conquer any trial or tribulation that you face, and He will do it with grace and mercy.

> *Sin is no longer your master, for you no longer live under the requirements of the law. Instead, you live under the freedom of God's grace.* (Romans 6:14 TPT)

The reason we have allowed sin to be the master of our lives is because we focus on the sin as opposed to walking in freedom. God wants us to be free of bondage and free from sin. I remember having a conversation with a friend and he was so dedicated to not have sex before marriage and making sure that he didn't fall back into porn, and hell bent on not looking at women lustfully. You ask, why is that a bad thing? Well, it's not bad at all, it's good you are putting forth the effort to do that. What I realized is that he was more focused on the sin and not focused on living and the strength of God that already lived in him. Put focus on your healing and put focus on living a free life. When you engulf your mind on not trying to sin, the temptation to do it grows because you're feeding it attention. You begin feeding it more attention than what it needs to have. Give it to God, and let it go.

Before I give you a prayer to say, I just want to say a little more. Be Healed!

Dear Lord,

Today I come to You and ask You to forgive me. Forgive me of my sin, and cleanse me of all unrighteousness. I know I have tried to do it my way for a long time and quite frankly, it has not worked. I know that You love me, and I know that you want the very best for me. I am sorry that I thought of You too small and didn't allow You to guide me on the path of good. I now know that You mean me no harm but to live a life of prosperity and happiness. I no longer want to live in unforgiveness. I no longer want to just be someone who passes pain on to other people or further generations. I want to be healed of anything that I have bottled in or let fester.

Lord, if there is anything that I need to forgive someone for, I pray and ask that You show me who, and show me how to forgive them. Holy Spirit, I ask that You come into my heart and show me the areas I have been hurt in and who hurt me. Give me grace and mercy as I go through the process of forgiving them. I do understand, Lord, that this is a process. I know it won't be the easiest, but I pray and ask that You provide me strength to get through it.

Lord, if there is anything that I need to forgive my parents for, I pray and ask that You show me how to forgive them. I know that my parents aren't perfect. Although I might have not felt all the love, or love at all (for those who don't know your parents or the other parent) but I know that You are a loving father and thank You for keeping me. I pray that my parents are healed from whatever traumas or problems they have that were passed to them. Heal them Lord and heal me.

Lastly, Lord, I ask that You show me how to forgive myself. I know I have beat myself up over and over for the things I've done or allowed to happen. I ask that You forgive me for not inviting You into the decisions that I made that caused major hurt and pain. I know I want to be whole, but I know that it will only come by submitting my will to You. I will no longer focus on my sin or mishaps but focus on the healing that was provided for me when You died on the cross for me. I trust You, Holy Spirit, to guide me through all truth and that I will be just fine. I pray that in my healing, those around me will benefit from it as well. I know my healing isn't just about me but those around me and those who don't know You.

Pray this scripture: "God, I invite your searching gaze into my heart. Examine me through and through; find out everything that may be hidden within me. Put me to the test and sift through all my anxious cares. See if there is any path of pain I'm walking on, and lead me back to your glorious, everlasting way – the path that brings me back to you." (Psalms 139:23-24 TPT)

Today I choose You! Heal me and renew me. Care for me and redeem me, Lord.

In Jesus Name,

Amen

6

MINIMIZE THE SCROLLING

W HEN IT COMES TO trending topics, there is not one more influential than social media. Today, social media is the middle of everything. We have many different platforms, such as, Facebook, Instagram, Twitter, Tik Tok, and other outlets. I have seen the good that social media can do. You have people who have built businesses, you have people who have gone viral and became rich, and you have people who just want to do good and encourage people to be the best person they can be. I truly believe that social media was created to be a good thing. However, as time has passed, I truly think social media can be one of the worst things that was ever created. The evolution of social media from AOL to Twitter, it has evolved into a monster that I don't believe will ever be able to be tamed.

LIKING YOUR WAY INTO WORTHINESS

I remember when I used to want to get all the likes and have all the followers and just wanted people to know who I was. I would post all my workout videos and show my body progress. I would vent about some personal things that I wanted people to know so they would feel bad or show some type of sympathy. I would maybe even delete a picture that a lot of people didn't like or pay much attention to. I would ask God, "how am I supposed to make an impact if nobody is paying attention to me?" I mean I would take a great pic and get ready to see all the likes coming through and shoot, maybe even the girl I had a crush on at the time would like it and I could slide in her dm's. Oh wait, am I the only one who has thought like that before? If you say no, you might be lying.

What I became accustomed to was looking at the other people who were putting their business on social media and I became jealous because they were getting all the attention and getting the attention from the people I desired attention from. I felt like I had to take a picture with my shirt off or be extra light skin and bite my lip (now I still do that from time to time.) I felt that if I posted my basketball workouts, I would get the respect of the other hoopers who did the same thing. The funny thing is I wasn't working out as hard as I could because I was making sure that whoever was filming me got the hardest rep I did. Or I would do a hard rep to make it seem like I did all my reps like that. Yeah, ladies and gents, I am just being real with you.

It's like when you go to the gym, and you see that one person who is in the mirror flexing and posing the entire time. I'm like bro or sis, "have you done a single workout yet?" I don't know if you all have heard the saying, "You can become what you hate the most." Well, I absolutely hated when someone was posing or flexing all the time because usually, they were in the way of the machine I was trying to use. But then you might see them on Instagram, and you see they have 10K followers. Your mind gets to wondering, "how do they have *this* many followers?" You know that you work extremely hard at the gym while they are just taking pictures.

Let's go a little deeper here for a little. While trolling others on social media, you might come across their relationship status. Have you ever looked at someone and their significant other and wondered how in the world did they get them? Better yet, how many have had friends and lowkey wanted their girl or guy because "they aren't being treated correctly" or you know the dirt that goes on and you can treat them better? Is that a little too much for you? Well guess what, I don't care I am just putting out real thoughts here folks. There might be a thought of, "If I just had one chance, I would give that person the world." These my friends are thoughts of the enemy. Having these thoughts can lead you into a place of darkness and acting out of character. There will always be people who post a lifestyle that is not real or not how they are making it seem to be. There are people who post these fascinating relationships who are being beat at home and behind closed doors and behind the camera. Men, there are women we have watched on porn that are forced to do that and are being raped and put through sex trafficking.

I bring this to your attention because the things we are using for pleasure, for our own "needs", can be someone's prison or downfall. I will never forget when a friend of mine was telling me how he was talking to this young lady, and they were getting close and exchanging certain things through text. He soon found out that the stuff that was being sent were things she was forced to do and was put through abuse, rape, and domestic violence. He said at that moment, he apologized to her and never turned back to porn or anything like that again. Something he was using for his pleasure, turned out to be a horrific life experience for the young lady. He said it brought him to tears to know he was "enjoying" something that he could never do to any woman because of the respect he has for women. It made him look at himself and at that moment, he knew he had to make a change and really repent for what he just now learned.

Again, I bring this to your attention because you don't know what you have used for pleasure that is someone else's deepest pain. When you are looking at women in lust and the things they post, how many of you even begin to think if that woman is being forced to do that or do you just equate her to a hoe. Do women or men post things because they just want the attention and validation, yes! But even then, there is always a story to the why.

Okay we got a little deep there and my apologies but hey, I hope you got something out of it and changed your perspectives on things. Back to the original point of looking at those who make it seem like their relationships are perfect, and their lives are just totally awesome. Being on social media, you can make your-

> **There is always a story to the why.**

self to be whoever you want to be. I mean forget the ones who stay out here catfishing people. We are talking about real life, day to day, I post every 5 minutes people. As this evolution of social media has grown, so has the thirst for satisfaction and validation. It's almost like if you're not popping on social media or not showing what you're doing in your life, you don't matter. The one thing I want to reiterate is, even if nobody sees you, God does.

I struggled with trying to be positive and post positive things to help people's mindsets and not get any type of notoriety. Then you see a post that says "F YOU B" and it has 1,000 likes. It wasn't that what I said was bad or not good, it was that I was relying on the likes and the popularity to fill a void that only God could fill. I thought having all the likes would make people see that I was a good person. I thought posting all the grinding and the hard work I was doing would validate who I was becoming. The truth is none of that did a single thing for me. Also, it was extremely exhausting! It was God that came in and said that He knows my name. It was God that came in and said He knew me in my mother's womb and that I would be great. It was God who liked me before any likes were created on social media. I mean think about it; would God create something He didn't like?

The saying "The Struggle Is Real" doesn't compare to the "Thirst For Validation Is Real." I know I used to try to seek motivation in everything I could. Good or bad, I would try to motivate myself through it. What I soon learned was that motivation is something that is temporary, and you can't use the same level of motivation to get you through life. Just how pain and hurt can be temporary. If you break a bone in your foot and you keep walking on it and don't allow it to heal, eventually it will never heal. I know a lot of people will use someone they lost for motivation and does that get them to where they want to be, yes it might, but what happens when you reach that goal or destination. Now you have to be able to last in that and the same motivation you used to get you there can't be used all the time to keep you there. You must progress in your journey. The same level of healing you had to do for one thing might take a whole new level in a different season of life. Don't rely on motivation but rely on the Lord to get you through whatever it is you need to get through.

When you ask someone to validate your parking, it means that wherever you are at, they will pay a portion of the customers parking.

At some businesses, it is like a reward for doing business with that company. I personally have never had my parking validated but I have gotten a ticket for parking in the wrong spot. Regardless of the situation, parking in the wrong spot or getting your parking validated, when it comes to life, either can be hindering.

PARKING TICKET

Let's go over the parking ticket first. You go to an establishment, or an event and you see it clearly says, "NO PARKING." You might look at the other cars that are parked there and you see that they have no tickets on their cars. You might think to yourself, "Oh I'll be good." You proceed with going to your event, having a grand time and then you come out to a ticket on your window. You become furious because now you have to pay for your blatant disobedience. You saw the NO PARKING, but you continued to park there, and you even have the audacity to even have a good time in your disobedience and pride. "Oh, nothing will happen to me, I'll be good." Then comes the blame game. "Well, the other cars didn't get tickets, why was I the only one who got a ticket?" Does it really matter if the other cars got tickets or not? You knew the risk of parking in the NO PARKING zone, yet you went on and parked there anyways.

How many of us have parked on social media, scrolling in the NO PARKING zone? There are people you follow that just lead you into temptation and delivers you to evil. It's not their fault, you just have no self-control, and you want to fill your tank with what they post. You might think I am just talking about following your favorite swimsuit model or favorite porn-star, but no, I am

> *Don't rely on motivation but rely on the Lord to get you through.*

talking about following those who put toxic thoughts into your head as well with their toxic quotes or rants. One thing I have noticed on social media, there is always a page to meet your feelings where they are at. I have seen many different pages that can relate with how you are feeling in the moment. So, we park our feelings on that page and allow what is quoted to enter your heart and plant a seed. You plant the seed of "F so and so, and get money," when you could be planting the seed of the Word which says:

> *I am convinced that my God will fully satisfy every need you*
> *have, for I have seen the abundant riches of glory revealed*
> *to me through Jesus Christ!* (Philippians 4:19 TPT)

Again, who knows, you might follow that one person who does tempt your eyes and every time they post something, you start feeling some type of way. The truth is you know the people who can turn you off your focus. You know the woman or man that you lust over constantly who just makes you shake and takes you there. (Y'all know what there means.) You know the pages you follow that make you feel like you can look better, or you have to change who you are or how you look in order to be accepted and validated. I am not saying that following those pages are bad, but if you park yourself in a zone that you know distracts you or gets you off focus or tempts you in ways that don't honor God or yourself, or even the other person you are lusting for, then yes, it's unhealthy.

What happens when you park in a NO PARKING zone, is you make yourself accessible to have to pay for what you ignored. When you get a parking ticket, you have to pay for it. Parking in the NO PARKING zone on social media does have a price. You might think it's meaningless scrolling and that nobody will know the thoughts that are going on in your head, but the Holy Spirit does. One thing I learned in growing up is when you have thoughts that take over your mind, at some point they come out in real life. They are no longer just thoughts that you conjured up, they now have become reality.

Some of the thoughts come out in relationships when you have lusted after a woman so much that you don't even know, and now you're in a real relationship, not a fantasized one, and you don't know how to decipher the real from the fake. You have watched thousands of MUA videos to get your make up on point and now because you don't look like how they said you would, you become sad and are in discontent.

I say all that to say when you park somewhere you know you're not supposed to be, you pay the price for what you got yourself into. Some get so turned on by what they see on social media to now they must have sex or masturbate. Some seek so much valida-tion in how they look or how people think they should look, that they will save a lot of money for someone to make them into how they think other people would like them. I see all the time people posting about goals of other people's bodies. Folks, when will we be our own goals? When will we just be who God created us to be no matter what anybody says, or how anybody feels? I know we might not be where we want to be, but God takes us to where He needs us to be and to where we want to be.

> *Being lazy is desiring someone else's life and not creating your own.*

We can't get lazy in our own lives for our own selves. Part of being lazy is desiring someone else's life and not creating your own. The spirit of comparison is dangerous and hindering in the path of your own life. As I stated in the previous chapter, you cannot run your own race while looking behind or to the side of you. I will add, you cannot run your own race while scrolling on IG and parking on other people's page.

Although God may know what your "NO PARKING" zone is, the other person that knows is you. If you know parking on a certain page is going to distract you, then don't park there. Go to a place of free parking or a place where you will pay for it, but at least you know you are safe. Also, parking in a no parking zone can get your car towed, and then you will really have to pay for it. We will correlate getting your car towed to something drastic and detrimental. Parking in that area can cost you more than you wanted to pay. For some people, parking in their no parking zones have cost them marriages, jobs, good opportunities, friendships, and even finances. The NO PARKING zone comes with many rabbit holes that can turn into debt and not just financial debt, debt of life.

VALIDATED PARKING

For those of you who have had your parking validated, that's cool! I always dreamed of going to stay at the Ritz Carlton and lean over the counter and say, "Um, yes may I have my parking validated please? It's the burgundy 1967 Mustang out there with the burgundy rims, and the cream interior, (all in a British voice). Also, charge it to my black card." I am just messing with y'all. I pray I never become that person. As you can see in my baby skit, I approached the counter expecting the place to validate my parking. I expected them to pay for something I placed myself in. I parked in a place that would cost, but I had the expectation that they would take care of it.

How many of us have placed ourselves in a situation and thought that something or someone would just take care of it? I have heard for years men say that when they get married that their porn addictions and desire to look at women lustfully would just magically go away. I have seen women over the years give up their bodies and have someone's baby because if they did, then the man would love them and stay. I have seen people get in relationships and automatically think that they can change the other persons ways and make them into who they think they should be.

You could be in a career and making all the money and because of that, you think the money will solve the family issues that you have. You think that cause you make good money, your wife is happy, or your kids should be happy because you provide whatever they want. Money does not take the place of quality time and intimacy. Just because you are now married doesn't mean that all the sudden you won't want to watch porn or look at women in a freak nasty way. The same thoughts you have before you get married or before you start making the money, are the same thoughts you will have when you get into it. That's if you don't work on those traits before you become hitched.

If you are only wanting money to have everything you want and to provide for everyone around you, that will be your mindset when you get the money. If you are only wanting to get married to have sex without the "condemnation" or the condom, then it will show when you do get married. I once heard one of my favorite motivational speakers say, "Just because you change scenery, doesn't mean your mindset has changed. If you don't change your mindset, then it will follow you no matter where you go, no matter what situation you are in." So, if you are only thinking that you want to get married because of the sex and you don't have to feel bad about doing it, then homie, you might not want to get married.

A lot of men do think this way, and they do believe that getting married will help their issues. Well, this is exactly why I am writing this book. The single season is the time to work out of those mindsets, as well as work your way into the mindset of Christ. Getting into something WILL NOT heal you of a struggle or issue. That's why

> *All you're doing is giving out broken pieces from a broken vessel.*

you see people hopping from relationship to relationship because each situation may look better but you never really took the time to heal from the previous thing. Now, all you're doing is giving out broken pieces from a broken vessel. Now you're expecting the next thing to put it back together.

Some of you may have heard this and some not but, God is the potter, and we are the clay. God puts us together and molds us into a product that lasts and is sturdy and will not blow up. How many of y'all took pottery class? When making your project, you had to make sure that you had enough clay to make it sturdy and you have to make it strong enough so that it wouldn't blow up when they put it in the fire to solidify it. It's the same with God! We must allow God to be the potter of our story, the potter of our healing, the potter of our strength. Many times, I have tried to be the potter of my own story and tried to mold myself into what I thought would keep me in the fire. When I entered the fire, I would either crack or I would blow up. When the broken product would come out and who knows maybe an arm fell off my panther I made, but guess what I would try to do? I would try to glue it back together. And not with the strongest glue, like gorilla glue, I tried to glue what was now solid stone, glue it with Elmer's glue. Did it work for a moment, yes it did! But when it was placed in a place it shouldn't have been like my backpack, it fell apart again. The glue that was there had calloused over piece I was trying to fix, and so now not even the gorilla glue would work.

Do you see what I am getting to here? When we allow God to mold our clay (ourselves) he creates a strong product that can last and won't need the glue of our own healing. I remember a panther I made when I was 5 years old, and today that panther is still up right, no cracks, no missing limbs, and a great piece of art. You want to know why? I had help. The teacher of the class helped me to make sure that the piece I was making was sturdy and would last. God wants to help us last and wants us to not crack or blow up when we meet the fire.

The fire might be many different areas for us in our lives. However, with God, when we meet it, He will keep us through it and when the fire is over, we come out like solid stone in whatever area it was.

Nebuchadnezzar was so furious with Shadrach, Meshach, and Abednego that his face became distorted with rage. He commanded that the furnace be heated seven times hotter than usual. Then he ordered some of the strongest men of his army to bind Shadrach, Meshach, and Abednego and throw them into the blazing furnace. So, they tied them up and threw them into the furnace, fully dressed in their pants, turbans, robes, and other garments. And because the king, in his anger, had demanded such a hot fire in the furnace, the flames killed the soldiers as they threw the three men in. So Shadrach, Meshach, and Abednego, securely tied, fell into the roaring flames. But suddenly, Nebuchadnezzar jumped up in amazement and exclaimed to his advisers, "Didn't we tie up three men and throw them into the furnace?" "Yes, Your Majesty, we certainly did," they replied. "Look!" Nebuchadnezzar shouted. "I see four men, unbound, walking around in the fire unharmed! And the fourth looks

THE PAST THAT COULD AFFECT MY FUTURE

like a god!" Then Nebuchadnezzar came as close as he could to the door of the flaming furnace and shouted: "Shadrach, Meshach, and Abednego, servants of the Most Hight God, come out! Come here!" So Shadrach, Meshach, and Abednego stepped out of the fire. Then the high officers, officials, governors, and advisers crowded around them and saw that the fire had not touched them. Not a hair on their heads was singed, and their clothing was not scorched. They didn't even smell of smoke! (Daniel 3:19-27 NLT)

So, you see here that God brought these three men through the fire: literally! As I said, there are different fires of life but if you truly trust God to mold you (the clay) into something amazing and something that will stand, when you meet the fire, not only will you come out complete, but the battles and the journey you are on, you won't even come out smelling like smoke. Oh, and the fourth man that was in the fire was God. So, the next point is, God will not place you in the fire and not be with you while you're in it. God was in the fire with those three men and that's why the king saw four. Don't think because you have some fiery situations in your life that God won't be in the fire with you. Allow God to be with you every step of the way. Even if you go in the fire bound and to be burned, God will protect you in the furnace, no matter how hot it is, no matter how you go in, He will bring you out! Then you can say, I AM VALIDATED!

AVOIDANCE IS KEY

Well, after all that Azlan, what does that have to do with social media? I will keep this plain and simple. Avoid the no parking zones and be validated by God and don't expect others to validate you. Also, don't seek out validation from others and don't feel the need to validate yourself by what you see others doing. My dad's favorite quote, "Don't allow someone's influence on you to be so great to whatever decision they make is yours." (Miss you dad). When you are scrolling and when you are paying attention to the lifestyle others are living, yes, it's easy to get caught up in the "I wish I had that" trap. Again, you are your own person, and you have your own story. Embrace your story and embrace your journey. Be the one that people want to scroll and waste time on because you are doing what you are called to do.

Don't allow social media to be a slowdown to your goals and dreams. Don't allow social media to tell you who you are or who you can be when God is sitting right there ready to validate you.

"Don't allow someone's influence on you to be so great to whatever decision they make is yours."

Don't get stuck on what someone else is doing and how they're living their lives. Truth is, it might not even be real how they're living, they're just giving you a false narrative. There will be fires of temptation, fires of comparison, fires of wishful thinking. However, if you allow God to validate you and you don't stay parked in the areas of life that get you off track, and you trust in the Lord with all your heart, I guarantee you, when you come out the fire, you won't even smell like smoke.

Dear Lord,

With all the distractions in the world today, I am sorry if I put them before You. I know that there are many platforms pulling me in different directions. I know that I have at times maybe wanted to receive the attention from everyone else but You. I ask You to forgive me for that. Forgive me for going to the phone before I went to Your throne.

I pray that You would be with me in every step that I take. I pray that I will not have to seek the approval or validation from anybody else but You. I will not seek validation from the likes or the comments I get, or don't get on social media. I will not rely on the validation from my parents on what they think is best for me but only what You know is best for me. Help me to not fall in love with the idea of things but to allow You to mold me into the way I am supposed to be. I want to live my life for You today and not for anybody else.

(For those who have children) Lord, I pray that You protect my kids when I am not around. I understand that there are many forces out to get our children and that the enemy is trying to get them by any means necessary. I pray You would give me the strength and guide me on how to protect my kids from the temptations of the world and from the distractions that are all around. I pray You show me how to raise my kids up in You and that the only validation that matters is from You and who You say they are. Show me Lord how to give my kids validation as well. Show me how to make them feel affirmed and safe

when around me. If I have sought out any validation that didn't involve You, forgive me. If I have shown my kids a way that hindered my relationship with You and taught them that they need validation from the world, forgive me.

(For those who desire to have kids one day) Lord, I pray You are preparing me and molding me into the man or woman that I am today for Your glory. I know that I may not have kids right now, but I thank You that you are preparing me to be the father or mother that I will be one day. I thank You for showing me how to be solid in You and helping me break from the mold of my past and cementing me into the mold of the kingdom. I thank You that in me seeking affirmation or validation, that I validate myself with the rich word of God. Because Jesus died on the cross for me, the price has already been paid and I thank You. I pray that You are helping me remove anything that can be detrimental to not only myself, but my kids in the future.

Thank You, Jesus, for finding me worth the cost of Your life so that I may be saved and validated in the kingdom. I now know that through You, all things are possible and that I don't have be dependent on the pressures of social media to be who You have called me to be.

In Jesus Name,

Amen

7

FOCUSING YOUR FOCUS

I REMEMBER IN PRE-SEASON WORKOUTS in high school, every year at least once, we had to run from Montbello High School to Pena Boulevard. Now for those of you who don't know where that is, it's about a 2-mile run. Some say well that's not too bad. Then we had to run the hills on the highway. We would run up and down, do defensive slides up and down the hills, back pedal up the hills, and oh did I mention it was straight dirt? Guess what else? None of us had our cell phones on us, therefore, we couldn't call our moms, or friends, or 911 for help. So yes, we had to run back to the high school after all that, in the heat! If you know me well enough, you'd know I hate the heat.

Junior years run was tough for me. Why? Because I was not focused at all. I was coming back from a winter camp with Younglife. Let's just say it was the best/worst weekend ever. I mad me good friends, I had fun, and I got my heartbroken all in the same weekend. Prior to the trip, I was very focused. I would finish my workouts and then go run an extra mile after we finished practice. I was in the gym getting up shots. If I couldn't get in the gym, I would walk to the park by my house and shoot around there with my homie Conrad. I mean I was doing the thing. I knew the upcoming year was going to be huge and so I had to be ready.

Going up to the camp, I had a good friend who I also really liked too! She was great and I just really cared for her a lot. Now I am not going to get into the details of what happened, and it wasn't anything crazy, but the camp was for people to find the Lord, and I was not trying to find Him, I was trying to find the key to my friend's heart. Let's just say I never found that key either. The purpose of the camp was to get closer to God and I had a different agenda. In a way, I thought by being there with my friend and God being there too, it can't get any better than that. However, getting closer to her was my priority and there shouldn't be any God's before God.

The issue here is that my focus was never on God in that situation from the start. It was on how could I make this work; how can I show her I am a good person? My thirst for trying to be validated by what she thought had taken over and I couldn't be a good friend to her like she was to me. Now, was I a good friend, yes I was. However, I never just was content with being her friend, I wanted more! You see, my focus was in a place of my own opinion and own knowledge. The other thing, whenever your focus is not on God and the Holy Spirit, things will become hazy and might put you in a place worse off than what you in were before.

After coming back from that trip I was hurt, I was confused, I thought I had done the right thing only to know it was not good for either side and more importantly, I was distracted and off focus.

TO BE A CHAMPION, MUCH IS REQUIRED

I remember almost being done with that run coming back from Pena Boulevard and about 2/3 of the way back to the school, I just stopped and was walking in the middle of the street almost. Cars were driving around me and honking yelling "GET OUT THE STREET!" I was so hurt and focusing on the hurt that I just didn't care. My coach was driving up behind me and saying, "you're almost done why are you stopping?" I just told him I was tired and couldn't go anymore and had done the best I could. Was that the best "focused me" could've done? Absolutely not. However, was that the best "unfocused me" could've done? Sadly, yes it was. When you are off your focus and are focusing on something that has nothing to do with the current circumstance or situation, you under achieve and you do not produce quality in what you do.

Coming back from the run, I looked like I hadn't eaten in days, hadn't tasted water or even seen any chap stick in my life. I went into the gym and just sat in the bleachers just moping and pouting. Now this was in high school and so of course I didn't tell my parents a lot of what was going on with me. But even when you don't say anything, most parents just know when something is wrong, especially if they are paying attention to their kids. My dad could see that I was not focused based off the time I came back from my run. Prior to the trip, as I stated, I was working extremely hard and so my dad knew something was up. He came and sat next to me and was just a father. There were many times I got Coach Doug as opposed to dad. I truly thank God for this moment because it was a moment I would never forget.

> **Dad:** *Hey G, How was the run? You seemed a little slower today than usual.*

> **Me:** *It was cool, I just got tired quickly.*

Dad: So, what happened up there at the camp this past weekend?

Me: Nothing too much. Just tried to relax and have as much fun as I could. Didn't sleep that much.

Dad: Oh okay, I see. So how is your friend?

Me: She's cool, I guess.

Dad: Yeah, that's good! But look G, I don't know what happened at that camp but whatever happened between y'all, you cannot let that get you off focus. You have a big year coming up and if you want to be a champion in this, much is required. You can't be who you want to be if you don't know how to focus and if you allow things to derail you. Your friend is doing what she's doing and more than likely ain't going to let you or anybody else get her off focus. Your focus has to be on you, for you. You choose what you focus on. God will take care of you, but you must stay focused!"

As I was sitting there listening, eyes swollen from crying, I realized that he was right. In that moment, my dad had to take off his coaches' hat and put on the dad cap for a minute and man did I need that. The part of him telling me that I choose what I focus on was huge and that is what we are going to talk about next.

YOU CHOOSE WHAT YOU FOCUS ON

Many times, we as human beings tend to focus on the problem at hand as opposed to the solution. There are situations that do need tending to, such as someone dying in your family or a friend or someone close. You would need to take the time to focus on grieving and allowing yourself to feel the emotions. Things you might not want to focus on so much is getting your hair or nails done when rent is due. You might want to focus on putting food on the table instead of planning a trip to Vegas or Miami for the weekend. You might want to focus on finishing your paper instead of scrolling the gossip and drama on Facebook. Again, you choose what you focus on.

It's natural to react to a situation that causes you to pause and say "okay, what is the priority here?" I can't tell you how many times I reacted to shoes that came out and bought them when I should've saved up some money. I told myself that I had to have these shoes, and never once did I have a real answer as to why I "needed" them. I knew back in high school, if you had shoe game, you were the man. Growing up, I never really got the shoes that I wanted to have or that everyone else had. However, God was good and throughout high school, I don't think I ever had to pay for a pair of shoes.

When I became an Assistant Manager at Finishline in 2018, I vowed to get any shoe that I wanted. I wanted to get all the Jordan's I could and then finally, I would be that guy! But you see, I had the same mindset when it came to shoes as I did in high school. Seeking validation through what was on my feet. I mean for those who know me best know that I don't even like feet. My co-workers would always say that I was working at the wrong place. I was so focused on what was on my feet, that other areas in my life were lacking focus. I was focused on what other people would say about my shoes and not focused on saving money to build a future and invest into my future.

I knew that some women loved a man with shoe game. Having a bunch of pairs of Jordan's means what? It means you have a lot of money and have style! Right? Naw homie… Not everyone with a bunch of pairs of J's has money. There are a bunch of people who have all the J's and no money. There are people who are more focused on their sense of style instead of the sense of living. Again, I was seeking validation from something that couldn't fulfill me. Focus in the wrong area mixed with a lack of self-control, causes debt and self-worthlessness.

What happens when you get the shoes and not the girl? What happens when you get the shoes and people keep walking past you? I know what happens when you get the shoes, and your stomach is growling. A lack of focus on priority keeps you in bondage. As I said, when you're focused on the wrong thing, it can cause you debt.

A problem I had was always eating out. On a real tip, if every time I ate out, I would go to the store and buy food to cook, I would probably be a millionaire right now. No joke! I lacked vision for things that would get me further, but I couldn't go further because I couldn't look further than my stomach. I love to eat, and I love to eat A LOT! The issue I had is I was focused on what my stomach was telling me and not what God was telling me. Because of me eating out so much, there would be times I wanted to go to a basketball camp or something but couldn't, and you know why, because I ate all my money.

I know some people who have focused on finding love and neglected their children. I know people who have been so focused on their careers to where they neglect their loved one. I know many people who have focused so much on an issue and not walked in the freedom that Jesus paid for, and yeah that person was me. I was one who would focus so much on a person that I would lose myself in the process. As I like to say, watering someone else's grass while mine is brown and dying. And can I tell you how exhausting that is? Let's just say, it's very exhausting.

Focus again can be dangerous depending on what you choose to focus on. If you are focused on everything and everyone else instead of what you're supposed to be doing, then yes you will be distracted and you will feel like you're stuck and not going anywhere. You will miss what God has for you if your focus is not on Him. It's like I mentioned earlier in the book about the Israelites; they were focused on the giants in the land instead of what God promised to them.

Who knows, God might have brought you the blessings and miracles, but you are focused on everything else around you and you don't realize what's right in front of you. I don't want to be too hard on you because yes, there are so many distractions and things to focus on. But you have to remind yourself to focus on what's yours, not theirs, yours. When we pray, we must be still and ask God to show us what to focus on. I know one thing God will tell you is to stay focused on Him no matter what. I remember asking God how do I focus on myself? I was in a place where I know I needed to just do me, but I really didn't know how to. God gave me the simplest answer I had ever received. He said, "You focus on yourself by focusing on me." One thing I did know how to do was trust in the Lord and go to Him in my time of need. I needed to focus on me, and he provides all my needs. Another thing He said to me was, "You need to build your prayer life on the basis of priority."

FOCUS ON THE ANSWER

Many times, we can pray for things that aren't a priority at the moment. You might be praying for God to make a way for you to get your hair did, but the rent needs to be paid and your kid needs clothes and food. You might be praying for you to win the raffle for the new J's to come out, but you have to pay your tuition for school. You might be praying for husband or wife but haven't stepped foot into the healing arena. Whatever it is you pray for, you must prioritize your prayers. There will always be something that is more important than something else.

> *Be saturated in prayer throughout each day offering your*
> *faith-filled requests before God with overflowing gratitude.*
> *Tell Him every detail of your life.* (Philippians 4:6 TPT)

So, you see, God wants you to tell Him every detail of your life. And although we want all of our prayers answered at once, it's one step at a time. Just like Rocky says on my favorite movie CREED, "One step at a time, one punch at a time, one round at a time." We must be still enough to get the answer. Ask God how to move in the answer we have received, and then do it. Every answer is not going to be a likeable answer, but when you're obedient, it will cause prosperity in every area of your life. It also causes you to walk in purpose.

You know what is most important in your life and what things you need to be done for you. I encourage you to focus and prioritize your prayers on that! When you learn how to prioritize, the things you want to do seem to become more available when you want to do it. *Focus on God and He will take care of your needs.* As Jackie Chan said in Karate Kid, "Your focus needs more focus." Focus on God and He will take care of your needs! God loves you more and knows the details of your desires, just be detailed with Him through prayer and seeking Him and make Him the priority and just watch how your Godly focus turns into miracles and wonders.

Dear Lord,

I thank You that You have kept me this far. I know that there have been many times that I have gotten off focus in life. I know there have been many times I have taken my focus off You, and I ask that You forgive me for that. I know that I choose what I focus on, and I know that what I focus on determines where I go.

I now know that in order to stay focused on myself and what I have to do for my life starts with focusing on You. I know that you, Jesus, were focused on what You had to do in your life for all the people. I thank You Jesus that despite the distractions, You knew that You had to do Your father's work. I know that I am that work and the project that You died for so that I could choose to live a life of freedom and not bondage.

I know I have been easily distracted many times in my life, but I always thank You for meeting where I am and bringing me back to You. Thank You for saving me from the distractions that could've been destructive. Just as David prayed to You when he got distracted and fell into temptation with Bathsheba, I want to pray that same prayer now and help me back on the right path.

"God, give me mercy from your fountain of forgiveness! I know Your abundant love is enough to was away my guilt. Because Your compassion is so great, take away this shameful guilt of sin. Forgive the full extent of my rebellious ways and erase this deep stain on my conscience for

I'm so ashamed. I feel such pain and anguish within me. I can't get away from the sting of my sin against You, Lord! Everything I did, I did right in front of You, for You saw it all. Against You, and You above all, have I sinned. Everything You say to me is infallibly true and Your judgment conquers me. Lord, I have been a sinner from birth, from the moment my mother conceived me. I know that You delight to set Your truth deep in my spirit. So come into the hidden places of my heart and teach me wisdom. Purify my conscience! Make this leper clean again! Wash me in Your love until I am pure in heart. Satisfy me in Your sweetness, and my song of joy will return. The places You have crushed within me will rejoice in Your healing touch. Hide my sins from Your face; erase all my guilt by Your saving grace. Keep creating in me a clean heart. Fill me with pure thoughts and holy desires, ready to please You. May You never reject me! May You never take from me Your sacred spirit! (Psalm 51:1-10 TPT)

Forgive me for all the sin that I have done with being distracted and not focused on You Lord, but focused on how I feel. I know my own feelings have gotten in the way but continue to set before me a clean heart to pursue. Thank You for Your grace and mercy!

In Jesus Name,

Amen

8

EMBRACING YOUR SINGLENESS

W E ARE NOW AT the part of what this book is all about: Embracing your singleness! We have gone through some of the parts that could hinder us from embracing your single season, and now we are going to go through how you embrace it and be okay with it. God wants you to prosper in every area of your life and especially in your singleness. We have to understand that the single season is the most important time of your life for every area of your life. I am slightly upset it took me so long to understand this but as always, God's timing is perfect and right on time.

One day, my Gi Gi and I were having one of our conversations which I love so much! I absolutely love our talks because there is always so much richness and wisdom in the talks. She asked me why I think I am single. Of course, I wanted to say because nobody appreciates me, and women don't know what a good man is if it slapped them in their face. But as I really sat and thought about it, I really couldn't answer the question. I was in a place of discouragement and on top of that, the enemy was working hard to make it seem like it was me.

When I say that the enemy was trying to make it seem like it was me, he was trying to convince me that I wasn't a good person, that I couldn't make a woman happy without sleeping with them, and that ultimately, I was the issue and not good enough. Now, none of that was true but the real answer that I received from the Holy Spirit is that it was me. I was not ready to be in a relationship. As my grandma and I dug deeper, I realized that I was more in love with the idea of a relationship as opposed to the process of being ready for a relationship. My Gi Gi has never been short of an encouraging person. She has the nickname "The Velvet Hammer." She gets that name because she does everything with a gentle and loving spirit, but you might feel like you got hit with a hammer after she talks to you.

At the time, I was living with my mom, I didn't have a job that could take care of a family, I didn't know how to save money or keep my car up to par, I was not on my own or nor did I know how to be. I watched my mom pretty much do majority of the work growing up due to my dad's health issues. When I was younger, I did see my dad work, I did see my mom work and they did well. When my dad's health issue took over his life, my mom did everything! And I mean EVERYTHING. I always wanted to help my mom out as much as I could but again, I was a young boy. I wanted to have fun when I could, and I was all about basketball and chasing my dreams.

On the flip side, I would see my grandparent's relationship, and it was always an example of what I hoped my relationships would be like. I watched my grandpa work, and my grandma didn't. The bills were always paid and there were always flowers on the counter and dinner on the table. They went on countless cruises multiple times a year and they just always seemed so in love (which they were). The thing that I always saw was that my grandpa was happy to do all that for my grandma. In his words, he believed God put him on this earth to make and keep my grandma happy.

As I stated in the first chapter, my grandparents were married for 28 years, divorced for 7, and then remarried and were together until my grandpa passed. But in those 7 years of separation, both my Pop Pop and Gi Gi had maturing and growing up to do, especially my grandpa. He went through a season of real singleness, and I could probably say loneliness. When my grandparents were divorced, my grandpa went through a rough time. He lost a lot, including his family in a lot of ways. My mom did the best she could to keep the relationship going, and they had a bond a lot of people will never get to experience. There was a time my grandpa was homeless and all he had was his van. My mom would tell me at times, she would drive around and just look for the van so she could with him.

If you knew the second half of my grandpa, you would never even know that he went through what he did. My grandpa has always been sharp and always classy. I mean prior to the divorce my grandpa had a great family, a great wife, beautiful children, my mom and my aunt Chaunci. You would think this man had it all, why would he throw it away? Back in the day my grandpa had the nickname, Candy Man. Why that name? He was sweet to the ladies. My grandpa always reminded me and everybody else of Billy Dee Williams. He had the charm and he kind of looked like him too. So, he had the game and the ladies loved Ronnie Calloway.

I remember a conversation my grandpa and I had, and I asked him what the most important season in his life was. He told me it was his single season. Not the season of not having a girlfriend but doing whatever you wanted. He said in the season when he was homeless and alone and had lost everything. He looked at me and said, "pay attention to what I went through so that you won't have to walk in my shoes." During the time that my grandpa was single and homeless, the Lord really had to work on him and work with him. My grandpa was faced with the reality that he had lost everything. My grandpa was always a hard worker and always a provider. He would say that he was always a better father than he was a husband. He loved his girls but would the girls have been there if it wasn't for my grandma.

My grandpa would tell me how sin was the root cause of his infidelity earlier on in their first marriage. So, yes, my grandpa was part of adultery. Nobody is perfect folks, but our God is. During that time of my grandpa finally living out his single season, he got it all together. He was able to get a job, he was able to get a place, and he was able and blessed to get my grandma back. Now, God had to work on my grandma too in some areas. When God told my grandma to listen to Ronnie Calloway, she straight up said no, no to God. But in her obedience, I can tell you now, it was the best decision she made.

My grandfather told me to embrace my singleness and to follow God so that the same mistakes he made, would not happen to me. We should not have to struggle or go through traumatic experiences to learn how to embrace our single season. Many of us have been single or chosen to stay single based off traumatic experiences that we have endured ourselves or seen others go through. Relationships have been made out to be a fear tactic in some ways. Also, relationships have just been pinpointed to just a boy and a girl thing. Relationships are formed all around in friends, co-workers, church members, the list can go on. We have been conditioned to think that the term "relationship" is a romantic thing. The term single can be mistaken for loneliness or being alone. But today, I want to give singleness a new meaning and put it in a new light.

ACCEPT SINGLENESS AND JESUS

The definition of embrace is, to accept or support (a belief, theory, or change) willingly and enthusiastically.

I chose that definition because it goes away from the embrace that most of us think about when we hear that word. Usually, when you think of the word embrace, you might think of; to hold someone or something close in one's arms, especially as a sign of affection. I want to break this down real quick. The first word in the definition is accept.

> When you become so independent that you become prideful, that's where issues can begin to form.

How many of us truly want to accept singleness? As I said before, singleness has been associated with loneliness way too much. Singleness can also be associated with independence and recklessness. You may think, "I'm single so I can do whatever I want with whomever I want to do it with." One thing I have noticed is that when you're single, you have the "stigma of being independent." Now, let me say this, being independent is not a bad thing at all. You need to be independent in a lot of ways when it comes to being single. When you become so independent that you become prideful, that's where issues can begin to form.

I know people who I've tried to compliment, and they can't even take a compliment. I think in a lot of ways today, independence has become a defense mechanism. Being independent keeps you from relying on someone else. Being independent keeps you doing for you. Again, those things aren't bad. But the question I want to ask is why are you so independent? Many times, being so independent has kept us stagnant in our faith with God. You won't rely on anybody else, so why would you rely on someone who you can't see?

In the single season, you want to keep your independence but when it comes to the Lord, you must give up your independence and become dependent on Him. This is the first step to accepting your singleness. You might have thoughts of, why am I still single or when will it be my time. When you accept singleness and give your independence to the Lord, he will show you what to do to get prepared. I remember hearing a sermon by Steven Furtick and along the lines he was saying if God told us exactly the day and time our significant other would walk in our life, why would we need to have faith. If God told us the exact date that we would get that dream job or get that car, why would we need to prepare or have faith.

The truth in this is we have to accept the Lord and His will, and the rest will follow. If you knew how it ended up, you wouldn't need to get ready. When you trust in what God told you He would do for you, the ball is in your court now. You continue to live life and not wait on a moment to start living life. Too many times we wait on a relationship to start traveling. We wait on a relationship to build a business or empire. Let me say this, it's okay to go on dates with yourself and take yourself out to eat. Don't wait to live life because someone is not with you to do it. That's where independence comes in handy.

I heard Michael Todd say that if God isn't enough, then no person ever will be. I will add to that and say if God isn't enough, then no job ever will be. If God isn't enough, then having kids won't be either. If God isn't enough, then nothing that you do or pursue ever will be. And if God isn't enough, then you won't be either. What I mean by that last quote is, God has so much in store for you. He has so much to get through you that needs to be shown to the world. I have a quote written in my bathroom that says, "The world is waiting on you to be who you're supposed to be." Your single season can't be filled if you are constantly looking at what's forward and not what you can do today.

> *Refuse to worry about tomorrow, but deal with each challenge that comes your way, one day at a time. Tomorrow will take care of itself.* (Matthew 6:34 TPT)

SUPPORT OF THE SINGLE SEASON

We went over how you have to accept the season you're in when it comes to singleness. It's like when you get a call, and you have the option to answer or decline. When God tells you that it is a time for you and Him to fellowship, become intimate, and for Him to guide you into purpose and calling, you choose to answer the call or decline it. Again, life is a choice in all aspects. The truth is, many of us have declined the call to singleness because we fear we will miss out on something, and we will talk more about that later in the next few chapters. For now, we are going to focus on answering the call to singleness and understanding how pivotal it is.

There are many seasons in our life when we go into different levels of life and try new things. In trying new things, we always want to make sure that we are secure, and we have the support necessary to maintain or see it through.

We might switch majors halfway through school because the original plan just isn't working, or you lost interest in it. We might be leaving a job where it was comfortable, and you had good relationships in your job but now you're going somewhere where you know nobody and it's a different field. Shoot, you might be leaving a relationship that wasn't all bad but because it wasn't progressing or going anywhere, you had to dip out. These are all examples of things that could happen or maybe could've happened to us already. No matter the journey, when we do take a leap of faith, we want to know if it's a safe leap. Will I be okay? Will I make good money? Will I make friends? Will I learn how to do things on my own as opposed of doing stuff with my ex?

These are all valid questions and questions you should ask yourself. However, these are all questions we ask ourselves but don't ask God. It goes back to how many times have we decided and moved forward and left God at the bus stop. It doesn't matter what avenue you are taking next in your life; you must find security in Him before you seek security in anything else. No job is secure when you are in the working field. Your best friend might be your boss and you might think that you are safe, but what happens when an employee comes in and does your job better than you? Now, if the boss is fair and a real boss and has morals, they would decide based off what is best for the company.

> God is always speaking, but are we listening and being obedient?

What good is it being in a relationship that is secure financially but everything else is floating about at sea? I have heard and seen many scenarios where a couple got together and stayed together because it was financially beneficial. But what about your heart? You may be able to get and do whatever you want but the attention, the affection, the friendship, the feeling safe with your emotions is all lacking.

When I moved to Tulsa, being honest, did I truly know if I was going to be safe and secure? The answer in my flesh is no but the answer when I trust in God is yes. God told me move to Tulsa. The thing we must understand is that when it comes to God, He will not lead your somewhere or tell you to do something if He will not provide or make you secure. This is not a thing to say I hear God better than you. That's not the case at all, but I do know that God is always speaking, but are we listening and being obedient?

There were multiple times when I was questioning if I heard God correctly and was I really supposed to move. Every time I began to have doubt, I would hear Michael Todd say in a sermon, "Move To Tulsa," and I knew that God was speaking to me and saying yes that was me, move to Tulsa. When I heard God say that when my dad passed, everything will be okay, it was God! When it comes to God, there's no security check, security card, no password, no fingerprint access, or safe that can come close to the security that God provides for you.

I think about the times I did sleep around or do things out of character and things that dishonored God, and how his shield of protection stayed around me. God's grace and his mercy are new every day, but again, we make the choice to stay in it or take ourselves out of it. Even when we are in God's presence, the enemy will still try to overstep his bounds and tempt you.

WILLINGLY SINGLE

I was listening to Myles Munroe recently and he said something that stuck out to me. He said when it comes to being single, it's not a "single problem," it's wanting to be single that is the problem. He also said that the reason he and his wife will never get a divorce is because they are both still single in marriage. What does that mean? It means that even in a relationship or marriage, you should still be your own person. Too many times we have put our focus on being in a relationship or married to where we have put our own lives on pause. We don't want to do certain things because it would be "more fun" doing it with someone. I remember for a time I was thinking I don't want to go on another cruise until I am able to do it with my significant other. Well, that was not the brightest thought, and I am glad I didn't do that. Going on cruises is something I like to do and gives me great joy. Why would I wait for someone else to do that?

Part of a sermon with Myles Munroe, he proposed the same question of what are you doing in your single season? The same question I asked earlier in the book. Are you becoming whole and doing all the things you want to do? Newsflash: You don't need anybody to do what you want to do! Putting your goals and dreams on hold is delaying your purpose in what God wants to do for you.

> *Are you becoming whole and doing all the things you want to do?*

I knew how it would eat me up in wanting to wait till marriage until I had sex but would fall easily because I didn't really want to give that up. It came to a point in my life where I had to decide about what was a priority in my life. It was like I wanted to follow God and offer up my issues, but I wasn't willing to. When we come to the decision of really being single for a season, you have to be willing to do it and be committed to doing it. God truly wants the best for you and speaking for myself, every time I listened, I prospered.

As I mentioned before, how bad do you want it? How bad do you want to experience life to the fullest and freest just for yourself? How bad do you want to be successful? How bad do you want to be the owner of your business? How bad do you want to be in a thriving and healthy relationship? Your prosperity is in the how bad do you want it. As my mom would always tell me, nobody else can want what you desire for you. So, with that being said, you must do the work ladies and gents. You must be willing to allow the Lord to show you the areas in your heart that need to be fixed and healed. You must allow the Lord to show you how to go from step to step. Our healing won't be a whole fix all the time. We have to take it pain by pain, trauma by trauma. It's not easy but it's worth it.

Some of us haven't experienced real life trauma or anything serious. And you know what, that is even more of a testimony if you ask me. I talked to a couple people who said they haven't really gone through anything like loss of a loved one or dealt with any traumatic experiences and that was amazing to hear. I don't want everyone to think that having a testimony means you have to have had something traumatic happen. The fact that God has kept you and shielded you from those experiences is a testimony. Keep on living and keep on preparing in life so that IF any trials and tribulations come, you will be prepared in the Lord.

BE ENTHUSIASTICALLY SINGLE

One thing I notice today is it seems that most people dread being single. People will say they enjoy their independence and love doing whatever they want. However, majority of the things they post are relating to being in a relationship.

Another point that Myles Munroe made was that being married is temporary. When we die and go to heaven, we will not be married in heaven. So, for those of us who believe that the end goal is to get to heaven and hear "Well done my good and faithful servant" why are we so indulged into something that is temporary? It seems to me that the things we seek most after are the things that are only temporary. Getting married won't get you into heaven. Becoming the richest person on the planet won't get you to heaven. Shoot, going to church every day and posting about Jesus every post won't get you to heaven. None of this will get you to heaven if your heart isn't in the right place.

I heard Michael Todd say in a sermon that people don't get to heaven because of their unbelief. Even if we were to take heaven out the equation and just talk about life here on earth; would you get anywhere in life if you didn't believe you could get there? I have the dream of getting to the NBA and thriving. Would it be any good if I didn't truly believe I could get there? Would it be any good if I wanted to have kids and be married if I didn't believe that I would be a good husband and a good father? Would it be any good if I wanted to start a business but didn't believe it could work?

I say these things to say, if you don't believe that you can truly be single and truly submit to God, then you don't believe in yourself to be the best person you can be. Even those who don't believe in God believe in something when it comes to being successful. We have to be passionate about our single season because it has so much to do with everything else that we do in our lives. How we respond in our single season will determine how our careers will go, how we become husbands or wives, how we become parents, how we interact with people, and also how we trust in God. The single season is the "blueprint" for how your life will prosper, decline, or just stay stagnant. As long as we are willing to allow God to create that blueprint, it will be an amazing one.

JUST TRY IT

You know the saying, "You won't know until you try it." Well, that is the same equation here. You won't know how great and pivotal singleness is until you try it and are okay and satisfied with it. I remember my Gi Gi telling me that I must be so content in the Lord, to the point of if I was single my entire life, that I would be okay with it. Of course, at first, I was like oh heck no, but I knew what she was saying. I know if God isn't enough, then no person, no career, and no situation ever will be. Your job won't always be able to provide you safety. Your man or woman won't always be able to give you the validation you need. Money won't always make you happy and it might temporarily, but it won't give you joy. Happiness is momentary and joy is everlasting.

My challenge to you is to embrace and enjoy your single season. For some of you reading this book, you might say "I've been married for years now." To y'all I say find what makes you joyful and continue to be single. Just because you are now married and have become one does not mean y'all aren't still different people. You may have learned to adjust to each other and are living life together, but you are still your first name, and your spouse is still their first name.

Another Myles Munroe gem is when he said that every couple's goal should be to be single in marriage. If you are a real spouse, you would want to first seek the Lord, and then support your spouse, and trust God. Never stop being who you are just because someone is in your life or you have moved into a new level of life. Being YOU is why that job called you to run their business. Being YOU is why your friends call you for advice or to be in your presence. Being YOU is why that person asked you on a date. Being YOU is why that person asked you to spend the rest of their lives with them. Being YOU is why Jesus died on the cross so that you could be free.

Be YOU and live for YOU. When you are engulfed with yourself and the Lord, the possibilities are promising and priceless. YOU + GOD = Everything else works out! Embrace God, Embrace YOU, Embrace life. Just try it!

Dear Lord,

I know through my single season; I have not embraced it like I should. I ask that You forgive me for focusing more on being in a relationship than I have building my relationship with You. Forgive me for dreading a season where You have tried to grow and build me into the person You want me to be. I apologize for doing things my own way and thinking that I know best. I want to experience all that You have for me and all that I can do for the kingdom of God. I want to be the best I can be in every area of my life. I know it won't be perfect, but I pray that I put forth a worthy effort. In all I do, I pray I do it as if You were right there in the physical watching over me. I pray that I don't do things halfway but that I do all things in excellence, and I become addicted to that. I pray that when I do mess up, that I get right back up and not rely on my own strength to make a way, but I use Your way and your strength. I know that Jesus died on the cross for everything that I have done, and everything I will do but I pray I don't use that as a crutch or an excuse.

(For those who are married) I pray that You show me how to be single again and that You show me how to be single in marriage. I pray You help me and my spouse to understand that although we are married, You still have things for us to do separately and that we can build a heart of support for one another. Bring back the dreams and aspirations that we had prior to marriage and allow us to rekindle the flame of our goals. I also ask Lord that You provide the provision and the means to be able to be

successful in our journey. I pray that we seek You in each step of the way and that we invite the Holy Spirit to guide us in all truth and prosperity. Lord, show me how to be willing to be single and that I accept the call on my life. I pray that I endure this season with gratefulness and that I am enthusiastic about it. Hold me through the process Lord and continue to grow me in Your word. Show me the truth so that I may be set free.

In Jesus Name,

Amen

9

YOU AIN'T MISSING OUT

Now THAT YOU HAVE accepted the call and chose to embrace your singleness, now you need to get in the mindset of persevering and not thinking you're missing out on anything. As the term states, FOMO, fear of missing out, you have to know when walking in obedience, that you are not missing out on anything. There are many topics and lifestyles today that can distract you from your purpose because you fear that you might be missing out on something.

Here are a few of those topics for me:

- I want to play in the NBA, but I am 28 years old.
- I thought I would be married at 23 years old, but I am still single and don't know who I will meet or what I am going to eat for dinner tonight.
- I want to start a business but there are many other businesses with the same idea.

- I want to be a father, and I want to grow up with my kids, but I am getting older and enjoying naps more and more.
- Man, I really enjoy sex, how much longer can I wait?
- The club looks fun

Those are just a few thoughts that came to mind when I felt I was missing out. It is okay to have different fun. I used to think that being a Child of God that I couldn't have fun, and everything had to be religiously motivated. When I say religiously motivated, I mean that you can't do anything without feeling that you are going to get struck by lightning. Now, everyone see's fun in different ways. Some people love going to the club, and some people like going to play bingo. Some people like going to amusement parks and some people like going to the museum. What you see as fun is what YOU see as fun.

You don't need everybody and their momma to do what YOU like to do. Now, what I will get at is when you're having fun, where is your mind and where is your heart. I knew for me, I had to stop going to the club and going to the dance parties because it would put me in a place of lust. I mean going to the party and seeing the girl you have been crushing on in a short tight dress just does it for you. It also distracts you and takes you out of discernment. Going to those parties are not only dangerous mentally, but let's be real, most of the time a fight breaks out or someone is hating on you. I never sought trouble but again, I am 6'7 so if anything pops off, more than likely, I will be one of the first people to be seen. If I try and run, the party is filled with short people in the way of me getting out of harm's way. Okay, maybe went off topic a little but y'all get the point hopefully.

When you are having "fun," is the fun you are having distracting you from your purpose and your calling? You see it all the time. You see a young man who is focused and on his way to greatness, and he meets a young lady at a party. Bada boom, bada bang bang bang bang bang, (Pops voice, R.I.P John Witherspoon) now they are expecting a child. That doesn't mean that either one of their lives is over, but it has definitely been altered.

One of the most tragic stories I've ever heard is the story of Len Bias. Len Bias was projected to be one of the greatest players to ever play the game. I mean up there with Jordan, LeBron, Kobe, Magic, and Bird. After finishing up college, Len Bias declared for the draft and was going to be a high draft pick. This was 1986, when the two teams that ran the league were the Boston Celtics and the Los Angeles Lakers. This particular year, the Celtics had the number 2 pick. "With the number 2 pick in the NBA Draft, the Boston Celtics select…. Len Bias out of The University of Maryland." Len Bias said that his dream had come true, and the Boston Celtics had just gotten that much better with an already stacked team.

One decision can be your last.

To celebrate Len getting drafted, he decided, made the decision, made a choice, to go have fun with some friends. Around that time, cocaine was running rapid. Not only in the streets, but in the professional sports as well. Len Bias made the choice to do cocaine with his friends and it would be the last decision he would ever make. Len Bias would die in under two days of getting drafted because of having a "little fun." He had his whole life set up right before his eyes and because of one decision, it took his life.

That is the point I want to emphasize; one decision can be your last. Peer pressure is real folks, and it has been the deciding factor to a lot of people's lives. It has been the straw that broke the camel's back. My dad's favorite saying which I mentioned earlier, don't let someone else's influence on you be so great to where every decision that they make is yours, serves to be true in this situation. God will always meet you where you are at, but if you are not careful, you can meet other people where they are at. You don't want to meet people at the graveyard.

The other thing is the choices we make don't just affect us. They affect everyone around us. Doesn't matter the situation; it can be the choice to do drugs. Doing drugs will affect your family, your job, your attitude and overall aura. Getting pregnant or getting someone pregnant will change both of your lives together or apart. Not seeking God in your life affects your whole life. There are people out here who's main job is to be a distraction and an assignment to derail you off the God given plan and track. We cannot give curiosity a say so in our deciding processes.

> [For being as he is] a man of two minds (hesitating, dubious, irresolute), [he is] unstable and unreliable and uncertain about everything [he thinks, feels, and decides]. (James 1:8 AMP)

We don't want to allow ourselves to be pulled back and forth. We don't want to be of the world and of God because it will not work. We have to make a decision today to be with God or not be with God. We have not moved forward because we have not decided. Do not let one decision you make be your last!

THE TUG OF WAR OF CURIOSITY

The definition time!!! I will provide a couple definitions of what *Curiosity* means. One definition says; the desire to know. The other says; a strong desire to know or learn something. There was one part that caught my eyes under the first definition. This part said, "an inquisitive interest in others' concerns," also known as nosiness. I thought that explanation was interesting because it says you are interested in others' concerns. Throughout this book, I have tried to emphasize the importance of focusing on you and your own goals and path. When it comes to curiosity, it's just another form of distraction and lack of focus.

One can say when I was a virgin, I was very curious. The company I was keeping was always talking about sex and all the girls that they would lay down. Some even made fun of me for being a virgin. There are good traits about being competitive and bad ones. I wanted to be the best at everything I did. Even if I wasn't good at it, I wanted to be the best at faking like I was good at it. For someone who didn't really like a lot of attention, I sure sought after it a lot.

I would see people get all the likes and comments on Facebook or Instagram and I really desired that. I thought maybe taking a few pictures with my shirt off would make women recognize me. I thought putting all my workouts online would help me get respect. Shoot, I even thought posting scriptures and positivity would get me more likes and respect. Yes, I have used God as a crutch in the past to get personal gain. My curiosity took me to places I never thought I would go and kept me in places longer than I wanted to stay and cost me more than I wanted to pay. Those are the words my Pop Pop would use all the time when explaining his testimony. It might not be word for word but along those lines.

What about for you though? What things have you been curious about that put you in a place of regret? There are many different facets of curiosity. You might see some food that looks good online and you're curious to try it. You might see a job that catches your interest and something you think you can be good at. You might see someone's wife or girlfriend who looks good, and you wonder what that would be like…. Oops, did I say that? Yes, I did say that! One thing I have noticed is when you are curious about the wrong things, there will always be an opportunity to act on it.

If you see someone drop their wallet or their purse, you could keep it or return it. You have the chance to do the right thing or the wrong thing. You have a choice in whatever it is. You also have the choice to take your curiosity in the right mindset or the wrong one. When it comes to curiosity, it's like life, we have to make a decision. The more we allow curiosity to fester, the more we progress or the more we torment. Why keep looking at a married woman lustfully when you know it's wrong to do that? Well, Azlan, nobody knows I'm doing that. Wrong homie, God knows and the Holy Spirit who lives in you does too. Why try to sabotage a friend's relationship because her man actually treats her well?

Again, God has a path, a plan, a man, a woman, a career, a dog, for YOU! Don't allow curiosity to take you down a path of sin. When you allow curiosity to control your thought process and your actions, you lose the ability to be discerning and make sound judgement. Just like Paul told us to take captive our thoughts (2 Corinthians 10:5), we must take captive our curiosity and submit it to the Lord as well.

> *We use God's mighty weapons, not worldly weapons, to knock down the strongholds of human reasoning and to destroy false arguments. We destroy every proud obstacle that keeps people from knowing God. We capture their rebellious thoughts and teach them to obey Christ.*
>
> (2 Corinthians 10:4-5 NLT)

We must prioritize the curiosity. We must make sure that our curiosity is lined up with honoring our Lord. When we come to the point of questioning if what we are curious about is a good or bad thing, that's when we take it to the Lord. We can't listen to our own thoughts sometimes. We have thought up thoughts that have clouded our discernment and now we think it's "following our hearts." I was talking to a friend one day, and they were stating how they are always trying to do the right thing. This friend is a nice person and sometimes would get taken for granted and taken advantage of. I told this friend that sometimes doing the nice thing isn't always the right thing.

I think how many times we have enabled friends or family members or anybody for thinking we were doing the "right thing?" It's the nice thing to want to help a family member out until they can do for themselves. However, after a while, if they are still not working and not trying to do for themselves, are you doing the right thing for them? I remember seeing a post one day when someone asked a homeless man how he became homeless. The man simply said he became homeless by doing everything for everybody else.

IS EVERYBODY ELSE GOOD?

One thing about missing out is, a lot of us miss out on ourselves by focusing on what everybody else needs. The name of this chapter is "You Ain't Missing Out," but if you continue with the mindset of catering to everyone else and not yourself, you will be missing out. It's like all the people who were so eager to get married and be in a relationship and now they're unhappy because they felt like they didn't explore what was out there. Or the person who didn't follow their dreams but their parents' dreams and now they hate the career they chose and spent years in school to get there.

I am so blessed that my parents supported whatever it was I wanted to do and not forced me to a certain profession or career. I do remember feeling burned out in high school though. My father was very ill majority of his life and most of my childhood was spent catering to him and his needs. Do I regret it? Not one bit. I am honored and blessed that I was able to do everything I chose to do for my father. It wasn't easy but it was worth it to know that I was able to serve him. Same with my grandfather in 2020. When he became ill, I wanted to be there to help him. No matter how tired or taxing it got, I was going to be there because I loved them both.

After my dad passed, I thought I was really going to be able to focus on just me. Then my mom lost her job, and I decided to leave college to come back and help her out. Now, did she "need me to," no she didn't. I remember telling my dad a month before he passed that when he went on, I would take care of my mom. So, when she said all this was happening, I didn't hesitate to come back home. I went to Otero Junior College back in La Junta, Colorado so that I would be closer to home and in reach for my mom.

When being at school didn't work out for me, I did come back home and begin to work. I wanted to continue to go to school but the situation my mom and I were in at the moment, I couldn't do that. Living with my grandparents I was strongly encouraged to find work. It was a tough place to be in because I felt that my dreams and goals weren't a priority and that I just had to make it happen. My grandparents were always supportive of me and wanted the best for me and never will I ever say they forced me to do something because they didn't. I always wondered if I had just continued to go after my goals and finish school where I'd be now.

Let me sum this up as best as I can. If I had continued to go to school, would I be in the NBA and have a degree now, possibly. But would I have the life skills and wisdom and perseverance I do now, probably not. I would much rather have learned what I did then to

YOU AIN'T MISSING OUT

have figured it out on a much larger scale. I thank God for the time of uncertainty and the times I felt like I was going nowhere. All God was doing was watering the seed of prosperity that I planted years ago when I said I submit to Him.

When my grandpa passed, I felt in my spirit that my training and learning was in a place where I could branch out on my own and give what I learned a try. I remember talking to my grandpa about moving to Tulsa and he thought that was a great idea. Upon his passing, I knew I would be moving soon but it was so hard to break from the mold of doing for others. A family member asked me what the hardest thing about moving would be, and my answer was doing for myself. I mean my mom just lost her dad, and my grandma her husband. I was the only one who really looked after them in our family, and especially my mom. I felt bad leaving so soon after such a great loss in the family. As I contemplated moving, God told me I needed to trust in Him. He reminded me how He has always kept my mom and grandma. He was keeping them even when I wasn't thought of. It was a new level of trust I would have to tap into but it's a level I know would be worth it.

The best part of being single is being single.

Upon moving to Tulsa, the first month was weird. It was weird to just do for myself and not have to go anywhere. If I wanted to take a nap, I could. If I wanted to sleep in, I could. If I wanted to not do anything all day, I could. In being on my own I realized I could work on some of the things from my past that I didn't take the time to do or that I couldn't really do at the time. One of those things was grieve. I never had the time to grieve my father's death. From the time he passed, up until May of 2021, I was on the go, go, go. Now that I was on my own, I had time to think, pray, and release.

God's timing is always perfect and even though I went 9 years without purposeful grieving, the time I now had to grieve was perfect. God placed amazing people around me here in Tulsa, and it's just the beginning. I now know that my dad and grandpa would be extremely proud of me.

The point is you have to take care of yourself. Nobody will ever know the best version of you if you are always focused on everybody else's needs. Also, if you are placing your needs around other people's wants, you will be exhausted. It is okay to say no! No is a complete sentence that needs no explanation. You don't have to go get lit every weekend. Take some time for yourself occasionally. The best part of being single is being single. People ask me all the time, why I eat by myself. I say because it's fun and it's also cheaper. But also, because I know one day I will choose not to have this luxury of being able to do things on my own. I want to be married and I want kids, so why not enjoy it now and do whatever I want and eat whatever I want, when I want, for cheaper.

Make yourself a priority and allow God to show you who you are and who you are in Him. Break yourself from the mold of others and mold yourself to the identity of Christ. I guarantee you that you will stand out more. God wants you to be so dependent on Him to where it's like you just jump off the cliff into His arms and His care for you. Is it easy? Heck no! But it's so worth it. There are times when I get discouraged, but I have to remind myself of whose I am and not who I am. Who I am in my own eyes doesn't deserve the life I have and that I am going to push toward. However, the man I am in the eyes of my heavenly father, is a man who is going to move mountains and lead the masses to the kingdom of God. How do I do that? I do it with excellence by taking care of me and making me a priority. It may seem like you are never in the right position to help the way you want. But allow God to place you in the right position so that not only will you be able to be blessed, but you will be in a place to where you can bless others as well.

You prioritizing yourself will give you the energy and patience to do for others. You truly don't want to be in a place where you don't like people or don't want to be bothered. Trust me I have been there and it's just not possible to be content if you dislike people.

MISS OUT ON THIS

As we have covered, you ain't missing out. Things that delay you from your God given calling or walking in purpose are things you want to miss out on. Only you and God know the things that distract you and keep you stagnant. Only y'all know what curiosities keep you distracted and going down the wrong path. You want to miss out on those relationships that will cause you pain and extra time on healing. You want to miss out on those jobs that don't honor you or God and keep you miserable. You don't want to be so focused on what everybody else wants or thinks, to where you can't think or do for yourself. You don't want to feel weird for taking care of you.

Again, prioritize you! Be content with just you and God. As my Gi Gi, told me, you have to be so in love and content with God, to where if you never got married, never got that dream job, never made it to the NBA, that you would be good and still prosperous. That's just where you have to be mentally because God will give you the desires of your heart (Psalms 37:4).

In the moments where you become discouraged, meditate on this:

> *But in the depths of my heart I truly know that you, Yahweh, have become my Shield; You take me and surround me with*

yourself. Your glory covers me continually. You lift my head.
(Psalms 3:3 TPT)

Don't miss out on YOU because you felt you would miss out on everything else. God loves you enough to where you will never have to miss out. Trust in Him, and embrace the journey, not the fear of the missing out.

Dear Lord,

I ask that You help remove the fear of missing out on things that aren't apart of Your plans for me. I ask that You remove the curiosity that would cause me to trip and fall. I ask that I seek You in your moves for me to make in my life. I ask that You be the main source to my curiosity. If I am curious about anything, I ask that it be about Your word and Your heart. As David was a man after Your own heart, I ask that I be the same. I pray that You would guide me into all truth, and that I will allow the Holy Spirit to do so.

I pray that I see myself as a priority and that I don't exhaust myself by trying to please everyone else. I pray my identity is found in You and not the opinions of the world or other people. I want to make you enough God and I know You are!

"I stand silently to listen for the one I love, waiting as long as it takes for the Lord to rescue me. For God alone has become my savior. He is alone my safe place; his wraparound presence always protects me. For He is my

champion defender; there's no risk of failure with God. So why would I let worry paralyze me, even when troubles multiply around me? But look at these who want me dead, shouting their vicious threats at me! The moment they discover my weakness, they all begin plotting to take me down. Liars, hypocrites, with nothing good to say – all their energies are spent on moving me from this exalted place. I am standing in absolute stillness, silent before the one I love, waiting as long as it takes for Him to rescue me. Only God is my Savior, and he will not fail me. For He alone is my safe place. His wraparound presence always protects me as my champion defender. There's no risk of failure with God! So why would I let worry paralyze me, even when troubles multiply around me? God's glory is all around me! His wraparound presence is all I need, for the Lord is my Savior, my hero, and my life-giving strength. Trust only in God every moment! Tell him all your troubles and pour out your heart-longings to him. Believe me when I tell you - he will help you! Before God all the people of the earth, high or low, are like smoke that disappears, like a vapor that quickly vanishes away. Compared to God they're nothing but vanity, nothing at all! The wealth of the world is nothing to God. So if your wealth increases, don't be boastful or put your trust in your money. And don't you think for a moment that you can get away with stealing by overcharging others just to get more for yourself! God said to me once and for all, "All the strength and power you need flows from me!" "All the love you need is found in me!" And it's true that you repay people for what they do." (Psalms 62 TPT)

I thank You Lord that your love and strength wraparound me and that I am safe in You. Thank You that I having undoubting faith in You and I pray it stays that way!

In Jesus Name,

Amen

10

PURPOSELY SINGLED OUT

> *We have become his poetry, a re-created people that will fulfill the destiny he has given each of us, for we are joined to Jesus, the Anointed One. Even before we were born, God planned in advance our destiny and the good works we would do to fulfill it!* (Ephesians 2:10 TPT)

POETRY IS ONE OF my favorite hobbies. I love listening to poems, I love writing poems, and I just love poetry! I love the creativeness that comes from poems. The way you flow, the different words that rhyme, and the feelings you get when you hear a good poem. You can hear the time and effort it took to write a poem when it is performed. There is creativity, emotion, and effort placed into poems.

I love how God treats His children like poetry. There is a uniqueness about every single one of us. Not one of us have the same fingerprint, and you know why, because God made us to be ourselves, not someone else. When He created us, he had care for us, and showed emotion when we do something. Whether it is good or bad, God shows His emotion toward His children. Effort has to be made when He thinks of us. That's why Jesus came and died for our sins, so that we could be made free and receive the grace we don't deserve. It's just like God to treat us like poetry. When you hear a good poem, you tend to hear a lot of things that make sense, things that come together. Whether they rhyme or not, poetry is an art that comes together and makes sense.

When we allow God to mold us, to be His poem, He lines things up to make sense. When you hear a poem and you hear words rhyme and match, God is using you to have things in order. When you are out of line with God, nothing will rhyme, nothing will make sense. Your life will be like a newborn baby who just came out with a mixtape. Things also take time and need to be polished, and word checked when you write poetry. God is the author and finisher of our faith. Time after time, I would try to take the pen out of God's hand. I would think that my story would be better. I do have wisdom, and I am smart, but I do not always know what's best for me if I don't seek council.

Sometimes that council will be my mom, sometimes my grandma, and sometimes my spiritual leaders, Mr. Eric Willis, Rayfield Whittington, or Carl Kennedy. The reason I seek them out is because they are submitted to God's voice and God's guidance. They will never tell me something that they haven't taken up with the Lord. Although they are great in my life and they keep me focused and encouraged, I always have to ask the Holy Spirit what am I supposed to do.

CHOOSE JOY

As I am writing this today, I broke down. This is a real open moment with y'all so get your popcorn ready. It's not all that serious but just to explain to you that the enemy comes to steal, kill, and destroy. However, our God has come to give us life and life more abundantly. I woke up feeling heavy and just out of it. It was one of those days when you just don't know why you feel the way you do. I got up and called my mom and told her how I felt. She told me to just take some time and fill my word tank up. As I am praying, the ceiling in my bathroom starts leaking and I am like what else can happen. Let's pause right there. I am a very encouraging person. If someone needs encourage-

If you don't go through something, how can you endure something?

ment, I am at the front door waiting to give it. Now, I have been doing this a lot lately. I have been pouring out my encouragement juice, however, I have not been filling it back up.

Do I read my word every day, I do my best. Do I pray every day, yes. But one thing I forget to do at times is worship the Lord for all He has done for me. Now, when you hear me say worship, a lot of you may think that I am talking about shouting and throwing your head back and crying and screaming Hallelujah. That is a form of worship, but the way you live your life is too. When I clean and I am thanking God for my place and my car, that's worship. When I am going back looking at what God has done for me in my life, that's worship. When I play ball or workout and include God into those, that's worship. Everyone has different worship and different ways to praise the Lord.

Many times, people think they can only praise the Lord when a miracle or blessing happens. Others praise the Lord when they are at a low point and don't know what else to do. They cry out needing a miracle and so they sacrifice their way to allow God to come in and move. Some people don't do anything at all. They are just content with just getting by. They are satisfied with just breathing. Today, I felt all those emotions. Let me tell you this; God has your back in every situation, no matter what it looks like. The enemy will try to get you to focus on the situation at hand, as opposed to the Lord and what He promised us.

How do you give God thanks when you look at your bank account and you have little to nothing and you don't get paid for another two weeks? How do you give God thanks when your health hasn't been the best and your mother was diagnosed with breast cancer? How do you give God thanks when your babies are hungry, and you have no food? The answer to all these scenarios is, you choose joy!

> *My fellow believers, when it seems as though you are facing nothing but difficulties, see it as an invaluable opportunity to experience the greatest joy that you can! 3 For you know that when your faith is tested, it stirs up in you the power of endurance. 4 And then as your endurance grows even stronger, it will release perfection into every part of your being until there is nothing missing and nothing lacking.*
> (James 1:2-4 TPT)

I don't care who you are, there will always be trials of some sort. God has always kept His promises and has always kept me. I had to go back today and look at what God has already done for me. I saw that He made a way for me to move to Tulsa. I saw my grandpa be excited to go to heaven before He passed. He kept me throughout the death of my father. He gave me strength when I had none. He healed me from diabetes. He wakes me up EVERY morning. Sometimes ladies and gents, we have to remind ourselves where God brought us from. Just like Tye Tribbett said in his hit single

"He Turned It, "If He did it before, He can do it again. Same God right now, same God back then."

There will be trying times, but if you don't go through something, how can you endure something? Many of us have gone through things and came out on the other side. Some have gone in the fire and didn't come out. Our hope and our joy have to come from the Lord who provides it freely. Can money, sex, alcohol, fame, and a relationship make you happy, yes it can. But what I have learned is chasing happiness is a momentous, temporary emotion, whereas joy is a lifestyle and a character trait. A trait many don't have, and many don't choose. But joy is a choice, and it will give you endurance and give you strength, even when you can't see it or feel it. God wants you to be swole in Him. He wants you to be swole in His word.

> *The grass withers and the flowers fade, but the word of our God stands forever.* (Isaiah 40:8 NLT)

You can say that people fade away, money fades away, relationships fade away, feelings come and go, but the word of God remains the same and stands strong, yesterday, today, and forevermore.

A WORK IN YOU

> *I pray with great faith for you, because I'm fully convinced that the One who began this gracious work in you will faithfully continue the process of maturing you until the unveiling of our Lord Jesus Christ!* (Philippians 1:6 TPT)

I am writing this part to offer some encouragement. I know many times you feel stuck and stagnant. I know there are times when you feel like you heard God wrong, and you just don't know where to go. God is a loving God and a faithful one. God wants the best for you, and He wants you to be prosperous in your life. I have been there many times where I asked did I hear God wrong. It wasn't that I heard Him wrong, it's just I went about it the wrong way. I know when I get off track, God has his ways of getting my attention. The way He gets my attention might not be the same way He gets yours, but He will get your attention. Again, you have the choice to answer the call or ignore it.

We all have our different goals and dreams. We have different morals and aspirations. Whatever that looks like for you is the work you have to do for yourself. The work that God wants to do in you is for those who don't know Him. It's not even really for God, it's for those who don't have a relationship with Him. A question I had to ask myself one day was when I am out and about and on my own, do I represent Christ? If I am out with my friends or family, would a stranger who doesn't know who I am, would they know that Christ lives on the inside of me? Well, Azlan, how would they know if they don't take the time to know me? Just like desperation, alcoholism, not washing your yams (aka butt cheeks), has an odor, so does the light of Christ.

This is an odor you always want to be around and smell. It's like when you give your girl a hug and her hair smells like mangoes, or when you hug your man, and he is wearing that cologne that you love so much, and you don't want to let him go. That is what the light of Christ looks like, and smells like on you. Sometimes you wonder why you haven't left that job yet, or why you haven't stopped messing with a friend who is toxic. I think God created the game of chess because that is how we are. He places us in the right positions for a reason. When you are in a place where someone needs to see Christ, God places you there for a reason. It might not be the journey you wanted to take, but you are there for a reason.

I remember going to Charlotte, North Carolina in 2019 for a basketball tryout. And man, when I tell you I was working my butt off for this tryout, I was. I was working out 3 times a day and going to work. I was determined to be the best I could be, and I was determined to make the team. During the tryout, we were running drills and getting warmed up. One of the guys in the tryout went down hard and twisted his ankle pretty good. He was out for the rest of the tryout because he couldn't walk. As the drills went on, it was time for the dunking drill. Every basketball player's favorite drill (I mean that's if you could dunk). I remember thinking I was going to do the cradle rock. It was one of my favorite dunks to do, and I mean hey, I am in North Carolina. I've got to pay homage to the great Michael Jordan. As I went up to do the dunk, I felt a pull in my groin area. Now, I still made the dunk, but now I was like dang it, I should've stretched longer. Mind you, I stretched for like an hour. When I landed, I felt more of a pull. I pulled myself to the side from the workouts and I went to stretch some more. When I finished stretching, I felt good enough to get back on the court and continue. My groin still felt a little tight but hey, I am at an NBA G-League tryout, I am not about to quit.

As I took off running to do the drill, I felt a pop in my groin. With the pop followed excruciating pain and I had to hop off the court. Never in my life had I felt a pain like that. I also knew immediately that I was done, and I couldn't continue. Fear immediately took grip as I felt that I had torn my groin. I went to the trainer, and he agreed that it was probably a tear. I left the gym and as always, I called my mom. I cried and told her what happened but said I still trust in God. Majority of the tears came from the hard work I put in and how ready I was to finally achieve my dream. But for some reason, I felt like I had to be there for a reason.

Remember the guy that got hurt in the tryout, well yeah, he was sitting out in the lobby where I was at. When I walked past him, he was in tears crying his eyes out. I limped over to him and asked was he okay. He said he wasn't good and couldn't imagine why God would allow this to happen to him. I felt his pain because I myself even asked God why now? The guy proceeded to say how hard he had worked to be ready for this opportunity. Again, I knew how he felt. He told me that he didn't even believe in God but this time he wanted to try it. In my mind, I am like "oh no," the one time this guy chooses God to help him, and he gets hurt.

How many times have we trusted in God and the situation got worse? I know for me, that happened a lot. And in that moment of getting hurt at a tryout, I could've walked away from God, but He needed me for a greater purpose then just myself.

I told the guy that I understood how he felt because I just injured myself too. He was a genuine dude and asked if I was okay. In that moment, I now knew why I was in Charlotte. I heard the Holy Spirit say, "invite him to know me." God wanted to use me to get to him because we were in the same place. God was able to use me as His chess piece to put me in position to take one of His children under his wing. I told the guy that God has something better for him and that you are more than a basketball player, you are a child of God. As the guy began to cry again, I could see a freedom in his eyes. Right then and there he accepted Jesus as his Lord and Savior. God used me to get to him because we were in the same predicament and could relate. I didn't get the glory, but God did. He was looking down saying, "checkmate."

In that moment of encouraging someone else, God was speaking to me through myself. I had to break free from the mold of being a basketball player and submit my way to God's plan. There are works in you that God has to get out. Again, some works in you might not even be for you, it could be for someone else. In being obedient to the Holy Spirit, it produces an endurance in you that will keep you all your life. You don't lift weights and expect not to get stronger. When you lift weights, there is always resistance. When you face various trials and tribulations, there will be resistance and there will be soreness and sometimes pain. Just like in working out, when you keep doing it, the soreness will go away, and you will be stronger. In life, when you keep pressing forward, and you keep choosing joy, the endurance you build will put you in a place of prosperity, no matter what comes your way, you will succeed.

THE REAL SUPERMAN

I remember when I was in 8th grade and God truly stepped in front of the enemies' attack to take my life. My family and I were getting ready for dinner and enjoying each other's company. I went into my parent's room to grab something for my dad. When I entered the room, a loud crack came from their bedroom window which was by the street. We lived on a corner lot and had the brightest yellow house on the block. The crack was extremely loud, and I ran back in the kitchen, and we all were wondering what it was. The blinds were closed so we couldn't see what happened to the window.

The next day when my mom opened the blinds, the whole window had been shattered. It looked like the window had been shot, which caused the loud cracking noise. My dad called the police to come investigate what happened. When the cops arrived, one of the cops noticed a hole in the frame of the window. What the cop soon discovered was a bullet lodged in the frame. The frame was no bigger than an inch and the bullet was right in the middle.

I looked at the bullet hole and looked at where I was standing in the room at the time of the loud crack. I was right in the path of where the bullet had been lodged. I think about how in the world did the bullet just hit the frame. Whoever shot, how did they not hit the window, but the little part shouldn't have even been able to be hit.

See the thing that a lot of us fail to realize is, God does the unthinkable. He does the things that don't make sense. God does the "that shouldn't have happened." Logically, there should've been no way that bullet just hit the frame. God saw a different purpose for my life and saw that I would be here today sharing this testimony. I praise God for seeing me fit to continue to bring other souls to the kingdom. I thank God for protecting me even when I didn't know I needed to be. I was in the comfort of my own home, somewhere safe, and the enemy still tried it. No matter where you are, continue to invite God in. Stay in His presence and allow Him to be the provider, the protector, and lover of your soul and life.

NO MORE ROOM ON THIS BOAT

This might be the most important part of this chapter. When you are purposely singled out, not everyone can go with you. This whole book is so you can focus on you, who you're becoming, and who God says you are. Many times, we will make decisions based off what others' say or want to do. You might want to go on vacation, but you may not want to go alone. You might want to go to a concert, but your man or woman doesn't want to go. You might want to go to a specific restaurant, but your friend doesn't have a taste for that. You will decide based off what others' can or can't do. I know people who have followed someone to a college because it's what they wanted. I heard a story about a girl who followed her boyfriend to a Junior College when she had multiple full ride scholarships to major universities. She ultimately did what he wanted and not what she had worked hard for.

When God has called you to a certain place, it might be just you that goes. I see all the time, people saying when I make it, we all going to eat. Also meaning, when I get big and make it, everybody around me is going to make it too. In saying that, you put a target on your back that most people can't live up to. You open the doorway for moochers. What are moochers? Moochers are people or things that leach onto you based off the potential you have or the potential of something to happen for their benefit. You might have had this girlfriend since you were in high school, and she has supported you all the way. You might have a man who has been there and supported you in all your endeavors. Those are people you hope to keep around if they are beneficial to your progress. However, there are people who will go all out and support you, wash your feet, bring you food, the whole charade, just to get something from you.

You might say, well Azlan, so and so been with me through thick and thin. That's awesome and I am so happy for you. You need people like that in your life. Even then, those thick and thins still may not be able to join you on your cruise to glory, because it's not their path to take. I cannot emphasize this enough of living out your purpose, answering your own call in life, and understanding that in your obedience, others' will be able to prosper as well. In your singleness, you have got to want to be whole and desire to be used by God. There will come a day when you have a companion to do life with, but don't rush into it. It is only God that I am writing this book because singleness was something I struggled with tremendously. I despised being single and that's just the truth.

When I understood how much I could accomplish in my singleness, I was even shocked. We have talked about it throughout the book: where is your focus? When you allow your single season to be focused on God, and doing what you want to do, you create an identity. Your identity is solidified in the joy of the Lord. When you get in a relationship, you have to put a lot of focus on the other person and their needs. In a lot of relationships, God has taken the back seat. You will not be able to put God first in a relationship if you don't know how to do it when you're not in one. We pray for God to bring us our spouse but don't pray that God will keep us preserved until the appointed time. We pray for God to bring us a Godly woman but haven't tapped into our Godly manliness. We pray for God to bring us a Godly husband but won't allow God to show you how to be a wife.

Even in relationships, there are tasks that God needs us to do that may not include your significant other. Doesn't mean they don't need to know about it, but it can mean that you will have to go solo on that particular mission. Don't leave the dock and then look back and say oh I forgot so and so, I have to go back. Going back means you are delaying your purpose and calling that God has for your life. When you have stayed on the boat of your calling long enough and when God sees you're ready and He can trust you, then He might call you back to grab some more people. You cannot go back for something that you haven't grasped yourself yet.

GOD'S PERSONAL STROBE LIGHT

When God is using you to bring glory to His kingdom or molding you into the person He needs you to be, there is a certain light that will follow you around. You know in the TV shows when someone is about to sing or say something important and everything goes dark but there is a spotlight? That is what happens when you say yes to God. The thing is, the light doesn't just show up randomly, it's always there, we just have to choose to step into it. I know I mention Michael Todd a lot in this book but it's because his visuals are so awesome. There was one sermon he did where he was saying we have to ask God how to get from here to there. He had a bunch of dots with light and areas that were dark. He said that you choose to stay in the light each step you take but that's if you choose to. You have to ask God how I get from here to there.

When you are wanting to propose a business opportunity, but you don't know how to speak it, ask the Holy Spirit and He will show you. When you are wanting to propose to your girlfriend, Holy Spirit will show you when the right time is to do it. It's okay to seek council from those who have been there, but you have to remember that what they did was for them. Whatever path they walked on, was for them. Your path and God's plan for you is for you!

God's light on you will always be present, it's just will you choose to be present in it. God many times has placed His light in my life in every area. There were times when I chose to step in it, and there were times I chose to hide in the dark areas. I was afraid of what would happen when my dark stuff came to light. Remember when I said God is a protector; well, if He invited you into the light, don't you think He is going to protect you in it? When God calls you to the light, He has a plan that will not only protect you but keep you in the light, if you so choose. The light of Christ is the same but in each strobe light, there is a difference purpose. One light might be for you to show Christ in your job. Another light could be for you to show Christ in your sport. I personally think that Christ needs to be more on the front lines of every area in life. In our government, in our friendships, our romantic relationships, our jobs, our parenting, our secret habits, the whole enchilada.

Why don't you be the example of what that looks like. You can miss a blessing for your life and someone else's if you aren't focused on you. We are looking and waiting for someone to step up and be a leader. We are waiting for someone to be a Moses, or a Joseph, and shoot some are waiting for someone to be a Jesus. The truth is, there won't be another Moses, Joseph, or Jesus. They were who they were. You are meant to be who you are. Times change and we need someone who knows how to speak the heavenly language for new times today. So, why don't you become that person? Be the person people can say, "yeah they really trusted in God." The people I mentioned earlier, they were just being them and doing what God told them to do. Joseph didn't look at Potiphar and say "oh I need to be just like him and do what he does to be successful." Daniel didn't stop praying and acting in his purpose because "they" told him to stop. There will be things that people have opinions on, but again, why would God speak to them about what He told you to do? Now if you choose to ignore what God is trying to tell you, then He might bring someone along to share wisdom and instruction with you.

You ask me, "so, how do you embrace being singled out by God?" I have a simple answer for you ladies and gents, you walk in obedience. When God reaches out to you, however that may be, are you willing to say yes? When God tells you to do something, do it! When God tells you not to do something, don't do it! It might not make sense but as the scripture goes, obedience is better than sacrifice.

What is more pleasing to the Lord: your burnt offerings and sacrifices or your obedience to His voice? Listen! Obedience is better than sacrifice, and submission is better than offering the fat of rams. (1 Samuel 15:22 NLT)

You see here it is better to be obedient than to take chances or sacrifice. When it says offering the fat of rams, just add that up to saying it is better than offering up all your money to the Lord and giving up earthly possessions just because you think God wants you to. Now, if those earthly possessions are causing you to drift away from the Lord, then you might have to make a sacrifice. In your single season, the Lord will expose the things you need to get rid of and the things you need to prioritize.

I love reading the stories of the bible when someone was "Singled Out." There are many stories that you can read, and I guarantee you, there is someone in the bible you can relate to. Here are some of my favorites. Please take out your bible or favorite bible App and read them:

- The Story of Gideon in Judges 6:11-39
- The Story of David in 1 Samuel 16:10-13
- The Story of Mary in Luke 1:26-34

Each person was walking in purpose when God reached out and said who they were and what they were going to accomplish. You see Gideon felt like he was the weakest of his clan. How could God call on him to save the people? God found him fit for the position, you know why, because Gideon was going to be obedient. And with Gideon, I loved his reaction and doubt. He kept asking God for a sign that it was His voice he was hearing. God answered every last request too. Because of Gideon's obedience, he was able to deliver his people from the enemy. God will call you out and single you out to fulfill His purpose, for His people.

David was herding sheep. The great King David who we all know as one of God's most loyal people. David was the youngest of his father's children. He wasn't even being paid attention to, and

Samuel heard God speak to him and say "yeah, that's him." You see, our obedience determines others blessing and prosperity too. Had Samuel been disobedient to God, David wouldn't be mentioned in the bible.

Mary, whew, Mary, Mary, Mary. Can you imagine what she went through? Being a virgin, not married, and then has to deliver God's child. She dealt with the looks and gossip from her own people. She had to endure the speculation from her fiancé Joseph. She was probably being called out of her name as well. To be in a situation where the situation seems impossible, and then you still have to trust in God, man, that's tough. Mary was built different! And again, on top of all that, you have to deliver the child of God. Talking about applying unwanted pressure.

God will keep you and will show you how to get through whatever it might be. These are just a few examples of people who were singled out. Were they perfect, no they weren't. However, they trusted in God and when they were called to purpose, they did it. I can't say they did it without hesitation because they all hesitated, especially Mary and Gideon. Shoot, Gideon kept asking for signs, even when he was getting clear answers. But just like what Gideon was doing, God still wants us to keep coming to Him and asking. Even when we do question God and are hesitant, keep pressing toward Him. It doesn't matter what you look like, how much experience you have, how many mistakes you've made, God will single you out and when He does, be ready to accept the call.

Again, this journey will not be easy by any means. Distractions will come, doubt will come, and frustration will come. When those feelings or emotions arise, take them to God and allow Him to move you step by step. Ask Him how to take each step in His strobe light and not hide in the dark. There will be times you will ask what in the world am I doing and why did I do this. But I can promise you, that it will work out. Embrace the times where God has called you to be alone. Embrace the times when it feels like you are ready to give up, because God is strengthening you, not breaking you. Stay in His light and allow Him to guide your steps. Allow God to Single YOU out!

Dear Lord,

I know many times I have run from Your strobe light. I know that I have been afraid to be singled out. However, I thank You for always having Your light available for me to step in. I apologize for not choosing Your light and hiding in the dark. I thank You for the examples in Your word that help me see that You have singled me out for a greater purpose then even myself. I ask that each step I take, that Your light, guidance and love are present. Forgive me for taking Your grace for granted and using Your mercy as an excuse to live recklessly.

completely with joy and peace because you trust Him. Then you will overflow with confident hope through the power of the Holy Spirit." (Romans 15:13 NLT)

I trust in You Lord, and I ask that You fill me with joy, peace, and contentment in You. I pray that I will search for You and that you will meet me right where I am. Help me to enjoy being singled out by You and I accept the call.

In Jesus Name,

Amen

11

GOD'S ENOUGH

A S WE WRAP UP this book, I want to just say this: GOD IS ENOUGH! We have discovered some areas where we have tried to take the lead and do things our own way. We have talked about the necessity to focus on ourselves. We talked about chasing and embracing our own journey. We talked about a lot in this book, but this here is the most important advice; allow God to be enough in every situation of your life.

I shared with you some deep stuff. Through it all, God was always too much in a good way. Whether it was in my feelings, or needing a blessing, or helping someone else out, God would always show up and show out. I told you about when my father passed and how devastating it was. But God! In this chapter I just want to honor God for who He has been in my life. I will share with you a few stories. I will share a bunch of scripture, but I want to give the respect where it is due.

MOVE TOWARD GOD

I remember when I was in high school, and my family was struggling. We had a hard time paying the bills. I remember the hot water would be off, the lights would be off, it was a rough time. We had to boil water to take a shower or wash up. Had candles all around the house to have light. As I like to say, it looked like a scary movie in my crib. Growing up in a life of poverty or lack, you learn to be grateful for things and the little things. When we were blessed with groceries and money to pay the bills, gratefulness would be evident in our household. Now, this is not to throw shade on anybody because I had the best parents, but they were not on the same page. My dad thought one way and my mom thought a different way. My dad liked spending money and my mom didn't. My mom wanted to always go to church, my dad didn't feel like it all the time. My mom felt I shouldn't be playing basketball on Sundays; my dad wanted me to follow my dreams. However, the one thing that was consistent was me.

I would see my mom struggle at times. Working and taking care of me, helping take care of my dad because my dad didn't value his health as much, my mom was Superwoman for real. I saw my mom do things I have never seen anyone do. There are things I am sure my mom did that I don't know about, and that's okay because I saw enough. I wanted to always help my mom out as much as I could. Majority of the help went toward my dad and there were times that I felt as if my dad didn't care or want to be healed from his ailments. Helping someone who doesn't want to help themselves is exhausting. Truth is, in a lot of areas, he didn't want to help himself and he became reliant on me and my mom.

My dad would have days when he went into a diabetic coma. There were days when he would get blisters on his feet and then cut his foot open. We would come into the house, and it looked like a crime scene. I remember one day the oven fell on top of him while it was on. I still don't know how that happened. The last year of my father's life, he lost strength in his legs and so he would just fall out in the street at times. When his legs gave out on him, I had to carry him to and from the toilet and so did my mom. These are just a few examples of what happened and the things we had to endure. When I look back to all the things we had to deal with, I don't know how we were able to get through that. But then again, I do. It was God's hand on us the whole time. In our weak moments, in our tiredness, in our ready to give up, God kept his hand on us, and His strength is what got us through. We were dealing with all that daily, and going to school and practice, going to work for 10 hours, and then coming home to that. Also, my dad was legally blind and so he couldn't see much.

I don't mention these things for you to feel bad for us. I mention them because through all that, God remained true. We never went without a roof over our heads, and we never went without food. In the moments we didn't understand, God was molding us into servants for His kingdom. If you can't serve someone you love, you probably won't do the best at serving anyone else. In serving other people for so long, I learned recently how to serve myself. When my dad passed, I knew the time I spent serving him would be attached to me forever. It now became who I was. I had to learn how to serve the Lord the way I served my dad. Serving the Lord is different. You see, serving my dad was taxing and exhausting but it was rewarding. Now, serving the Lord is different.

For all that I require of you will be pleasant and easy to bear.
(Matthew 11:30 TPT)

In serving people, you can get worn out. When you serve the Lord, He says that everything He requires of us is pleasant and joyful, and it's easy to handle.

Although it was taxing serving my dad, I had the Lord in me. Therefore, I was able to handle it because of the strength that was holding onto me. Were there times when I got tired and felt like I couldn't do it anymore, oh most definitely. God places things and people in your life to keep going, keep on fighting the good fight, and building perseverance.

In your single season, I pray you don't have to go through the experiences I did. But I can say that I was put through the fire, and I came out on the right side. I could've cursed God, I could've taken my own life, but God said "Azlan, I ain't done with you yet!" I thank God for those times, because I would not be who I am today had I not gone through those times. Could I have tried to go around them, yes, I could've. I am grateful that I didn't go around but I met those trials head on. God will never give you more than you can handle, and truly believe that. If you are going through something you feel you can't handle, call on Him so he can help you.

MOTHER BOOGLET

This section is about my mom. Now, my mom has been the greatest example of love I think I have ever seen. For someone to stay and serve and care for someone who didn't want to help themselves, that's real love. When you see someone stay in something they didn't deserve, that's love. To go through everything she has gone through, and still love the Lord daily more and more, that's love and that's trust. How do you stay with someone who is in and out of the hospital, someone who really can't do for themselves, and raise a teenage boy? You must have love people. How do you boo your son when he has his first dunk in a game and scream "you dunk like a girl?" It's different love, but still love. During the time of my mom doing everything, we built a bond that is unbreakable, especially after my dad passed. We relied on each other so much and made sure that we both were good.

My mom is literally like my best friend. I can talk to her about anything and man, she is just such a great blessing. When she was diagnosed with breast cancer, the first thing that came to mind was I am not going to do anything but be encouraging to her. I am pleased to say that she is healed from that. Still there were days when I would break down because she is the only parent I have left, and I can't imagine life without her. But I also had to level up my faith in God. It's easy to have faith in God when that other person has the same expectation. I am one who doesn't like to think about the possibilities of anything negative. That's exactly what I do, think positive and talk to her in that way. My mom has helped me so much and I pray that God will bless me enough to one day be able to bless her abundantly with all she can ask or think.

ENTER HERE

God's presence is always and forever present. Again, we make the choice to enter in it, or stray from it. I see a sign people post on their Instagram's that say, "I Love It Here." That is where we have to be in our lives. We have to love it in God's presence. We must ask God into our daily lives. No matter what you're doing, God wants to be a part of it. You might ask God what to wear that day, He will show you. If you ask God which way to go to work, He will show you. Invite God into all your activities.

You want to be able to be so attached to God, that you won't forget Him no matter where you go or where you are.

God's presence is always and forever present.

149

You can be a concert and it's loud and the base is hitting you in your chest and you can't even hear yourself screaming, but you can still hear the voice of the Lord. I remember being in a club, music is loud, girls dancing, you can smell alcohol, weed, the whole enchilada, but I remember feeling like it was time to go. It was a feeling I couldn't ignore. I grabbed my homeboy and said "hey man, it's time to go." When I got home, I saw on the news where there was a fight that had broken out, and they started shooting. A couple people were shot, but no deaths. When I found out who was shot, it happened to be one of my homeboys. I didn't see him that night, but he was shot in his leg. He is doing just fine today and living a blessed life. The Holy Spirit will speak to you, but again, you have a decision to make.

When you enter in God's presence, He will protect you and keep you safe. Whenever I go out, as I stated earlier in the book, I say a prayer that says, "make me invisible to the enemies' tricks and plots." Doesn't mean that the enemy isn't out there looking for someone to devour, it just means being in God's presence, He will show you the path to take or not take, the conversations to keep building on or the conversations to cut short. He will remind you to do something. That's why the word says be sober minded.

> Be well balanced (temperate, sober of mind), be vigilant
> and cautious at all times; for that enemy of yours, the devil,
> roams around like a lion roaring [in fierce hunger], seeking
> someone to seize upon and devour. (1 Peter 5:7 AMP)

I don't want to elaborate too much more but I just wanted to tell you that God loves you and His love, and His presence is enough. In your single season, you must allow God to mold you. Remember God is not breaking you, but He is breaking you from the mold of the world and the opinions of other people. He wants you to be cemented to His love and His path for you. He wants His light to shine through you so it can reach those who don't know Him. Your single season is the most important time of your life. You might want someone to get money with, but there is much richness and wealth to be had in your single season that will cause even more wealth and richness when you do find the one God has for you. Also, don't think wealth and richness has to just do with finances!

Ladies, don't draw unwanted attention to yourself by telling the whole world what you are doing or who you are becoming. That is between you and God. I understand you want to show your body progress but keep that between you and God. As the song says, "What the enemy meant for evil, God turned it for good." Well what God creates for good, the enemy tries to turn it to evil. Don't give men a reason to lust after you. Allow God to give you the validation you seek and need. Let me be real with you ladies, I don't care how saved a man is, seeing skin distracts us. Also, your husband is coming. Don't post all the quotes and relationship goals that you want to have or the work you're doing to be a great wife. Keep you to yourself and you will be glad that you did.

> Be willing to be made low before the Lord and He will exalt you! (James 4:10 TPT)

Fellas, we have got to do better. We want a good woman but feed into the bad parts of them. We look at them lustfully, we keep our options open so we don't get hurt, our deepest secrets are embedded in what a woman can do for us. Fellas, allow God to be your source for all things. I know we get horny but watching porn and masturbating isn't doing anything but driving a wedge in between us and God, and eventually, your future wife. Ladies

God's light on you will always be present, it's just will you choose to be present in it.

SINGLED OUT FOR PREPARATION

too! Men aren't the only ones who have that problem. Be the man that God has called you to be. Don't wait until you're married to start working on your lustful habits, your porn addictions, your spending habits, your lazy moments. Work on it now so you won't have to bring unwanted and unneeded baggage into your God ordained relationship.

To everyone who needs to embrace your singleness; spend more time with God then you do on social media, with your friends, and doing for other people. One thing I have noticed in my generation is that people want a quick word, or a quote they can live off. Again, motivation or quick words are temporary, but the word of God is everlasting. It's okay to post the scriptures and sermons that have motivated you or spoke to your soul. But have you received and grasped the fullness of what was said? Or have you just read the one scripture and been like, oh, that's it right there. What I have learned is that in order for you to get the whole meaning of that one scripture, you have to read the whole chapter. Why go to a buffet and only eat the hors d'oeuvres when you have overflowing steak and sides and salads and desserts? You have everything you want and need right there at the buffet but settle for the hors d'oeuvres. It is the same in the word, you have buffet of things to choose from and you can get all you want. And guess what? When you are full there is still plenty of food left. Get my point? Get the word for you first before you try to put it on other people. You can't give what you don't have or understand.

This last part will be just scriptures you can meditate on to focus on yourself and build yourself up in the word of God. I want to end this on the right note. The word of God is life. The word of God is love. The word of God will help you through ANYTHING. The word of God singles you out so you can have you own book of the word. It is continued word and continued prosperity from those who came before us. Write your own book of Azlan, the book of Tyrone, the book of Shenehneh, the book of Karen, whatever your name is, write your own book based off the word of God. The last thing I want to say is, you can do this! There were many times I didn't understand why I was single but now I know that it has to do with a far greater purpose then just myself. It has to do with my future generations and those who struggle with singleness. In my obedience to God by writing this book, I believe singleness will have a different light and that you choose singleness and enjoy it. With that being said, thank you for getting to the end, thank you for supporting, and now embrace your singleness and embrace being singled out by God! It's time to get prepared.

Peace, love, and hair grease!

> *Get the word for you first before you try to put it on other people.*

FINDING YOUR IDENTITY IN CHRIST

Be willing to be made low before the Lord and He will exalt you. (James 4:10 TPT)

Simply join your life with mine. Learn my ways and you'll discover that I'm gentle, humble, easy to please. You will find refreshment and rest in me. For all that I require of you will be pleasant and easy to bear.
(Matthew 11:29-30 TPT)

Be cheerful with joyus celebration in every season of life. Let your joy overflow! (Philippians 4:4 TPT)

And without faith living within us it would be impossible to please God. For we come to God in faith knowing that He is real and that He rewards the faith of those who passionately seek Him. (Hebrews 11:6 TPT)

Don't be obsessed with money but live content with what you have, for you always have God's presence. For hasn't He promised you, "I will never leave you, never! And I will not loosen my grip on your life!" So we can say with great confidence: "I know the Lord is for me and I will never be afraid of what people may do to me!"
(Hebrews 13:5-6 TPT)

It is the Lord who directs your life, for each step you take is ordained by God to bring to you closer to your destiny. So much of your life, then, remains a mystery!
(Proverbs 20:24 TPT)

This is my command – be strong and courageous! Do not be afraid or discouraged. For the Lord your God is with you wherever you go." (Joshua 1:9 NLT)

Trust in the Lord with all your heart; do not depend on your own understanding. Seek His will in all you do, and He will show you which path to take. (Proverbs 3:5-6 NLT)

"For I know the plans I have for you," says the Lord. "They are plans for good and not for disaster, to give you a future and a hope." (Jeremiah 29:11 NLT)

We can demolish every deceptive fantasy that opposes God and break through every arrogant attitude that is raised up in defiance of the true knowledge of God. We capture, like prisoners of war, every thought and insist that it bow in obedience to the anointed one. (2 Corinthians 10:5 TPT)

When you go through deep waters, I will be with you. When you go through rivers of difficulty, you will not drown. When you walk through the fire of oppression, you will not be burned up; the flames will not consume you.
(Isaiah 43:2 NLT)

"But forget all that – It is nothing compared to what I am going to do. For I am about to do something new. See, I have already begun! Do you not see it? I will make a pathway through the wilderness. I will create rivers in the dry wasteland." (Isaiah 43:18-19 NLT)

Go ahead and make all the plans you want, but it's the Lord who will ultimately direct your steps. We are all in love with our own opinions, convinced they're correct. But the Lord is in the midst of us, testing and probing our every motive. Before you do anything, put your trust totally in God and not in yourself. Then every plan you make will succeed. (Proverbs 16:1-3 TPT)

And don't allow yourselves to be weary in planting good seeds, for the season of reaping the wonderful harvest you've planted is coming! (Galatians 6:9 TPT)

Put your heart and soul into every activity you do, as though you are doing it for the Lord Himself and not merely for others. (Colossians 3:22 TPT)

Pour out all your worries and stress upon Him and leave them there, for He always tenderly cares for you.
(1 Peter 5:7 TPT)

Trust only in God every moment! Tell Him all your troubles and pour out your heart-longings to Him. Believe me when I tell you- He will help you! (Psalms 62:8 TPT)

For here is the way God loved the world – He gave His only, unique son as a gift. So now everyone who believes in Him will never perish but experience everlasting life.
(John 3:16 TPT)

ABOUT THE AUTHOR

AZLAN WILLIAMS WAS BORN and raised in Denver, Colorado where he graduated from Montbello High School and then received a full ride basketball scholarship to Tuskegee University. Azlan attended Word Up Life Changers Ministries in Denver and loved being around family and friends. Azlan has many talents that he enjoys putting to use. A few of those are cooking, playing basketball, and playing the saxophone. He also loves to smell good!

He was raised by his mother Rhonda Williams and his father Douglas Williams who passed away in 2012. Azlan believes his biggest purpose on earth is to encourage those who don't feel adequate or relevant. He wants to show how much God loves those who do or don't know Christ. He truly tries to be the example of God's love based off of how God has shown Azlan that He loves him! Azlan is currently a tutor for Restoration US and creator of Walking Testimony Clothing.

CONNECT WITH AZLAN
Facebook: Azlan Williams
Instagram: @kingazlan116